The Writer's Idea Workshop

Includes more than 300 prompts

The Writer's
Idea Workshop

How to make your good ideas great

Jack Heffron

WRITER'S DIGEST BOOKS
CINCINNATI, OHIO

www.writersdigest.com

Visit our Web site at www.writersdigest.com for information on more resources for writers.

To receive a free weekly e-mail newsletter delivering tips and updates about writing and about Writer's Digest products, register directly at our Web site at http://newsletters.fwpublications.com.

07   06   05   04   03   5   4   3   2   1

Library of Congress Cataloging-in-Publication Data

Heffron, Jack
  The writer's idea workshop: how to make your good ideas great / by Jack
  Heffron.
    p.   cm.
  Includes bibliographical references.
  ISBN 1-58297-217-6   ISBN 1-58297-279-6 (pbk.)
    1. Authorship. I. Title.

  PN147.H365   2003
  808′.02—dc21   2003053531
                                                                        CIP

Edited by Michelle Ruberg and Rachel Vater
Designed by Sandy Kent
Cover by Chris Gliebe
Production coordinated by Sara Dumford

Acknowledgments

Many thanks to Meg Leder for her help in developing this book and to Rachel Vater, who helped it to production. Thanks to the sales and marketing folks, whose amazing efforts on my first book led the publisher to want another. They are: Joanne Widmer, Phil Sexton, Mary Poggione, Steve Koenig, Howard Cohen, Jennifer Johnson, Laura Smith, and Jennifer Conrard. Thanks to Julia Groh, Donya Dickerson, and Brad Crawford for their help and good fellowship. Also, a big thanks to Anne Bowling for her invaluable advice and inestimable patience. Thanks to Mary, Joe, and Anne Marie Heffron for being my loving family. And thanks, finally, to Sheila Bender, Meg Files, and all the people who have attended our annual Colorado Mountain Writer's Conference in Steamboat Springs. You have been a source of inspiration and nourishment.

About the Author

Jack Heffron is the author of *The Writer's Idea Book* and co-author of *The Writer's Guide to Places*. He is a freelance writer and editorial consultant. His nonfiction has appeared in many magazines, including *ESPN—the Magazine, Oxford American, Utne Reader* and *The AKC Gazette* and was recognized in *Best American Travel Writing 2000*.

His fiction has appeared in literary magazines. He is a former editor of *Story Magazine* and speaks at writer's conferences across the country.

Table of Contents

116 | Part III
Idea Parts

177 | Part IV
Better Ideas

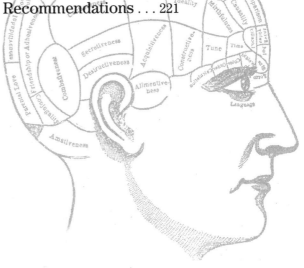

Introduction

When you were young, you made up stories. You invented characters and situations and perhaps you had a running saga in your mind, an imagined world with its own rules, its own conflicts and rivalries, and heroes. No matter what happened in your "real" life, no matter how powerless you felt, no matter how confusing or arbitrary or unfair the forces around you seemed to be, in your imagined world, you were the hero, perhaps even the omnipotent being to which your characters were faithfully devoted.

You made up these stories, because they were fun, or empowering, or offered some type of emotional haven. They made you feel good. You probably can remember where you made up your stories, such as while lying on your bed or while walking a path in a grove of trees near your house. Perhaps you used the sway of your backyard swing to launch your stories.

As an adult, the demands of the practical world made the story world more difficult to access. It also might have weighted those stories with demands beyond providing fun, exploration, or safety. As adults, we insist that our stories be more than fun. They must be good. And the proof that they are good is publication. To be published, we must learn what there is to know about strange new forces, known as agents and editors, who themselves bow to the omnipotent force known as "market trends." Before we know it, our stories, and our reasons for imagining them, have changed. Having moved away from the source of our imaginative energy, our stories lose a bit of their zest. They seem flat or mechanical. They seem trite or sentimental or manipulative. Sometimes they simply stop appearing in our minds at all.

Before you stop reading this book, let me assure it's not about ways of getting in touch with your inner child. We won't be generating ideas by spilling a tub of Lego's onto a floor to recover our lost innocence. Not one of the prompts suggests that you build A Model of My Creative Self out of pipe cleaners and pinecones. I am in no way qualified to round up the inner children of a bunch of writers, even if those children are spray-painting dirty words on my sidewalk.

I can recommend, however, that you recall your early days as a story-teller and keep those feelings in mind when you sit down to write today. Remember the sense of play, the sense of safety, the sense of secrecy, the sense of joy. Remember that writing is supposed to be fun. If you're doing it for a living, of course, fun isn't your highest priority, but even when you're writing a marketing brochure on deadline, approaching the task with a sense of play will produce better results. This advice must seem obvious. And yet, it's easily forgotten.

My older son—he's thirteen—reminds me of the story-as-play time in my own life. He likes to develop stories in his mind while shooting baskets. Sometimes he'll explain a scenario or two but usually he won't. And he insists that he shoot alone, that he can have the concrete back-yard court all to himself. If a hapless father is granted the privilege of shooting on the same court at the same time, the father must adhere to a strict vow of silence. No questions about how was school or what's your story about or did you poop-scoop the yard yet. My son doesn't aspire to be A Writer, and he's never mentioned hoping to publish his stories. He just likes to think about them, to spin out the dramas in his mind and sometimes to write them on paper. As I shoot along side him, I often think about ideas for articles and books, ideas I can sell, ones that I evaluate for marketability, for their suitability to various publications. It's a bit humbling.

Beyond the First Spark of Inspiration

To get ideas for stories, you need to recover the sense of play, the sense of joy and discovery that writing once had for you. However, the focus of this book is not on sparking that first idea. Instead, we'll spend much of our time looking at what to do *after* the first gush of inspiration. You can find a number of books on sparking ideas for stories. I've even written one myself. These books perform a valuable service to writers. But that first gush, if you'll permit me to say this, is the easy part. Any-body can gush. The hard part is turning that gush into something wonderful on the page, something that approximates the glorious explosion of beauty we first imagined.

Writers in movies are big on the gush part. We see them struggling with a project and *suddenly*, while they're walking down a crowded street or making a small purchase at a store, the light bulb goes on. They dash home. Cue the orchestra. A mighty thunder of strings and timpani resounds while a montage shows us the writer's fingers blurring across the keyboard, eyes frozen on the monitor screen. In the morning, the writer emerges, exhausted and bleary-eyed, The Masterpiece finished. For the most part, I hate movies about writers. There's just not a whole lot of physical drama to show on the screen, and so the moviemakers fudge the truth.

As writers, we have these thrilling moments of inspiration, no doubt. But most of our work is written one step at a time, not from a single sweeping epiphany but from a number of small bursts of inspiration. We look for ways to sustain the initial idea, explore its possibilities, allow it to shift and change, ride its energy, fight through its rough spots. This book is about doing all of those things. I believe this is where the real writing occurs.

In part one, we'll look at some strategies for igniting the initial burst of inspiration, but we'll also discuss ways of keeping the rush of creativity flowing as you develop the idea into a piece of writing. You might end up with a finished draft or simply sketches and outlines. The goal is to move the idea from your mind to the page.

When you have words on paper, we'll move to part two, where we'll investigate ways of assessing your ideas. It's important that any type of critical thinking be done only after you have something on paper. And the critical thinking we'll do is not a matter of deciding whether the idea should be developed or discarded. Instead, we'll experiment with ways of evaluating and exploring the possibilities of an idea, allowing it to move around and shift its shape. Too often we try to harness an idea, to understand intellectually and control it before it's ready to yield its own freedom.

In part three, we'll break a project into its basic elements—form, structure, voice, and so on. We'll discuss ways of using each element as a source of further ideas, how each can expand the possibilities of your story. We'll also look at how each element can block your progress and how you can break through the block.

In part four, you'll find many ways to troubleshoot your manuscript and to get a stalled project moving again. You might also use this section to push a piece in a new direction or to see the possibilities for your piece from a fresh perspective.

You can use the book to carry you through a project from beginning to end. Or you can focus on a chapter that speaks specifically to a situation you're facing in an on-going project. Or you can open to any page and pick a prompt to seed your imagination, to begin a new project or simply to warm up before diving into an on-going one.

The chapters are short, and they are designed so that you can read each of them quickly. They include advice and instruction on the focal subject, as well as questions to ask yourself as you move more deeply into your ideas and projects. At the end of each chapter, you'll find prompts to help you move back to the page. You need not do them all, of course, and you need not do them in any order. Choose the ones that speak to you. Ignore the rest or come back to them later.

I believe that books of writing advice are valuable and can inspire as well as offer instruction that can save you a lot of time and trouble. However, they cannot replace the time you spend actually writing. Don't use this book or any other as a substitute for writing. You'll learn the most meaningful lessons about the craft through your engagement on the page—by writing. For that reason, I hope you'll use this book as a *work*book. And as you do the work of writing, I hope you'll keep in mind the sense of play you used when writing and storytelling were simply a great adventure, a place of excitement and freedom, when it supplied a keen sense of connection to yourself and the world around you.

Part I

You've Got An Idea

Chapter One

First Thoughts About Writing and Ideas

You're at a party, a family get-together or a gathering of friends and neighbors. You're standing at the food table, grazing a bit, perhaps speculating to yourself about the ingredients in the brownish pâté, which seems to be a coy mélange of ground liver, cinnamon, and sand. At that moment, you're approached by a stranger who you learn is a friend of your neighbor's cousin. You chat for a moment before you hear a common statement:

"So, I hear you're a writer." This is followed shortly by a blushing admission that he or she also is interested in writing and perhaps dabbled a bit while in college. You're interested, of course. It's always good to meet someone else interested in writing. And then you are told, in a dramatic tone, that he or she has (cue the terrifying pulse of Hitchcockian strings) *an idea*.

Sometimes it's a really bad idea. Other times it's a good one. Either way, you're going to spend the next twenty minutes hearing all about it, and you feel pretty darn sure that the idea will never find its way to the page. It will be talked about at parties and thought about on drives to the office or during particularly dull Little League games. But that's where it will end.

Almost anywhere you go, you can meet someone who has an idea. Getting an idea for a novel or memoir or screenplay or children's book or whatever area you're exploring is not all that tough. The tough part is bringing that idea to life on the page, sustaining its magical elements through the long grind of completing the piece. The tough part is generating ideas that expand and complicate and develop the initial one.

In this first section of this book, we'll look at ways of handling the tough part. We'll assume you have the initial idea, even a plump file of initial ideas. My first bit of advice in making an idea work is to explore it on the page as quickly as possible. Get something on paper or in a computer file. It can be a bare-bones description, a list of character names, a bit of dialogue that could set the lot in motion. It needn't be much. The important part is to have started, to have given the idea a life outside your mind and, with luck, a life that won't be squandered in idle party talk.

When I have these chats at parties, I'm engaged by the fact that the person would like to write. I'm concerned, however, by their desire to talk through the idea before beginning to write it. This desire reminds me of a line Wyatt Earp allegedly said to Ike Clanton, his Tombstone nemesis and the man who sparked the famous gunfight at the OK Corral. Clanton was wandering all over town earlier that day and throughout the previous night, boasting about how he was going to kill the Earp brothers. When Earp confronted Clanton directly, he said, "You talk too much for a fightin' man, Ike." And he was right. When the guns started blazing, Ike fell to his knees and begged for his life before making a quick getaway.

When I hear people talk at length about their idea, I find myself thinking, "You talk too much for a writin' man." (Even when the speaker is a woman.) There can be several reasons why they talk about the idea. First, if they talk about it, they don't have to go through the headache of committing it to paper. Immediate gratification! Or, they want to know if the idea is any good. They won't ask this question directly, of course. But it's implicit. My advice—to you, often not to them—is to not talk about the idea until it has a life of its own on the page. Furthermore, no one can validate or invalidate your idea, especially if it's not yet on the page. Ideas are everywhere. A good idea is a start, but it's not yet worth much discussion, and any judgments about its relative worth are premature.

The Need for Validation

When I speak at writers conferences, often I meet with a dozen or more attendees in 15-minute sessions, during which I critique a manuscript that has been sent weeks before. Usually the attendees have paid too much for the thrilling opportunity to meet with a *real* editor-slash-writer, and they place far too much weight on everything the god-like figure (in this case, me) says to them. In many of these meetings, I feel sure they'll walk away disappointed, because they seek something far more than comments on the piece they've submitted. Sure, that's nice too, but they're really looking for the answers to two questions:

1. Is this thing any good, and is it worth the time I'll have to invest to finish it?
2. Am I any good at writing or am I wasting my time?

Like a wise psychologist my replies are frustratingly ambiguous. I don't supply the simple, direct answers they want, because in many cases those answers call for judgments that no one other than the writer can make. A publishing professional can assess the marketability of an idea or project, though not in a foolproof way. (Think of all the best-sellers that were rejected any number of times before finding a home.) An agent or editor can supply an informed opinion based on trends in the marketplace and can say if the novel is too short or the subject too obscure or the intended audience too narrow to make the project easy to sell.

But no one can tell the writer if the project is "worth pursuing" any more than the psychologist can say, "Yep, your marriage is beyond repair. Call your lawyer on your way home from my office. Furthermore, you're never going to resolve your anger issues, and the personal demons haunting you will make your life a hellish torment until the day you die."

Each of us has to answer the questions by ourselves.

Is this project worth pursuing?

What do *you* think?

Do I have real talent, or am I wasting my time with writing?

What do *you* think?

I'm not trying to over-complicate the issue. Some apprentice writers think such responses are willfully oblique. There's a clear, straight, obvious answer, but the Real Writer/Editor/Agent isn't confessing, because the apprentice is not a member of The Club, where such mysteries are revealed, usually at the Tuesday meeting. Trust me, there is no such club, and those answers aren't being withheld. Those writers looking for The Secret, that elusive Rosetta Stone of Great Writing will be disappointed. They will search in vain and be constantly frustrated. Or they will become the type of writer—and surely you've met at least one of them—who is perpetually having "the breakthrough." The big one, in which all becomes clear, rendering all they've done to that point meaningless and launching them into a new stratosphere of accomplishment and success.

Developing as a writer (and, for that matter, as a person) is much more a matter of hundreds, even thousands, of small steps, of tiny breakthroughs. The mindset of seeking a single simple answer goes against the very nature of creativity in any field. People who look for the one magic key that will unlock the answer door tend to be people who oversimplify situations and are inherently lazy. Complications are, well, complicated, and so they espouse the theory of simplicity. They seek the simple and obvious solution. Often these people do well in sales and politics. You may have had a boss who thinks this way, and I hope for your sake he's part of your past, not your present. In fields where real answers are sought, where solutions are found incrementally in a series of small epiphanies, we must avoid such reductive solutions.

The answer to question number one, therefore, is impossible for anyone other than you to answer. Like any good psychologist worth his pipe and notepad, I usually respond to it with questions of my own: How invested are you in the project? Do you still feel passionate about it? Have you worked on it for so long that, in a way, you've outgrown it? Could you walk away and forget it? Are more engaging projects begging to be written? Is there something frightening or daunting about the project that is compelling you to want to run away from it?

Sometimes an idea has served its purpose and is no longer of interest. It was begun long ago, and it's been worked to death. It no longer speaks to who we are now. And yet, we are hesitant to let go. We've grown attached to it. We've put so much time and energy into it that would be wasted if we just let the project go. Or we simply need permission to move on.

If you can't quite consign that project to the "Learning Experience" file, place it in the "Masterpiece on Hold" file. You're not trashing the piece, but you're allowing yourself to move on. Taking this approach, says John Gardner in *On Becoming a Novelist*, can free your other projects. He tells the reader of the magnum opus he worked on over the course of years but invariably shelved. Knowing it was there, that his Work of Genius was incubating, allowed him to begin and complete other stories and books, which he was able to free from the burden of needing to be masterpieces. They could be what they needed to be. Consider this approach an option for the project that's clogging your time and interest. You may even want to put it somewhere in your workspace where you can see it. You know it's there. You'll return to it someday, when you are in the emotional or intellectual place where it can speak to you again. For now, other projects await.

Ha Jin, whose novel *Waiting* won the Pulitzer Prize a few years ago, struggled with his first novel for more than fifteen years. In the interim, he published three collections of poetry, three collections of short stories, and two novels. After completing each of these projects, he returned to the first novel. It was published in 2002 and is titled *The Crazed*. While interviewing him for a magazine article, I asked him if he'd had a breakthrough that allowed him to finish it.

"No," he said. "For many years I picked it up and put it down, and after so many revisions, I was finally able to finish it." He described the process after the first months of inspiration as "drudgery." But the story wouldn't go away. It haunted him. And so he continued to pursue it.

On the other hand, sometimes we remain fully invested in a project, and we want to pursue it, but we need this desire validated by someone "in the know." If that's the case, trust that the project is speaking to you at some important if mysterious level. You may not be able to justify your persistence to your writers group or your family or even to yourself. But if your intuition tells you to persevere, then follow it.

The Larger Question

To respond to the second question, I will say that some apprentice writers have more talent than others, no question. They have a natural facility for language or for storytelling. Some are naturally funny or poetic or observant. Some have a way of harnessing their fertile imaginations to create wonderful characters and energetic stories. The vitality they bring to every aspect of their lives explodes onto the page. Some are very disciplined. They adhere to a strict schedule of writing and thereby are productive. Some are well educated and bring a wealth of knowledge and erudition to any project. Some are well read and have learned from the masters. They know what works. They can hear the sound of good writing. Some have a deep well of compelling experiences to draw upon for material. They have led fascinating or exotic or painful lives, and by simply stating in a clear way "what happened," they create powerful stories. Some are tenacious. They want to write well or to complete a project or to publish successfully, and nothing is going to stop them. They are not deflated by rejection. They keep trying.

All of those elements, and more, can be mixed and matched in nearly infinite combinations. We are blessed in some areas, weak in others. And so, for anyone to say he or she knows you'll make it or you won't, that you're a real writer or you're not, is ridiculous. I went to school with brilliant writers, the stars of the program, who haven't written a word in years and probably never will again. I was in a writer's group years ago with a woman who had a certain gift for language but absolutely no knack at all for telling a story. The rest of us in the group waded through page after page of the various novels the writer was working on, and despite some lovely turns of phrase, the stories ranged from dull to incomprehensible. But that writer rose every day at five o'clock and wrote till seven, before leaving for a full-time job. Every day. She took her laptop on vacation with her, so she wouldn't miss a writing session. I recently bumped into a member of the group, who told me that the writer was working on a new novel that "everyone thinks is really good."

So who's to know and who's to say? If you want to write, you'll write. Some will succeed more quickly than others, for the various reasons mentioned above. Don't rely on anyone to say, after reading some pages from your manuscript: "Oooooh, baby. You're the real deal." That means nothing. For years I spoke at a handful of writers conferences every year, from coast to coast. And at every conference there were at least a dozen writers working at a level that would allow them to make it. There were a few who were particularly gifted. And there were many more who were at various stages of their apprenticeships and who, with persistence, could achieve a level of mastery. So being the real deal is no guarantee of success.

Conversely, your "expert," having read your piece, might respond with, "Ahem. Well. This certainly is, um, unique. Say, you know you might try switching from writing stories to working with polymer clay. The lady next door makes the cutest little people out of that stuff." Again, this opinion means nothing. You may still be working toward an engaging voice on the page. You may not have found your best material. You may still be sharpening your skills.

If you burn and yearn to put words on paper, keep doing it.

And avoid labels. When you get that first spark of inspiration, withhold judgment. You don't yet know the true nature of the idea. Don't think it through to its most obvious conclusion. Don't begin composing your Oscar acceptance speech. Know that the process is just beginning.

What you can do, and what will be the focus of many chapters of this book, is explore your ideas, play with them, assess which ones interest you most, which ones have that certain fire of inspiration and which ones interest you for reasons that eventually will make them difficult to complete in a satisfactory way. You'll cultivate a keener instinct about your ideas, and we'll look at many ways of doing that. Do know from the start that the decisions, finally, will be your own, and they will arise from you. We won't be assembling a magical Assessment Grid that you can use to rank the relative worth or potential of your ideas. Of course, if you happen to know of such a grid, I'd appreciate a quick e-mail about it.

Questions to Consider

1. Do you have an idea you've been noodling in your mind for a while? What aspect of the idea keeps it so alive?

2. Are you holding yourself back from developing an idea into a draft by doubting its worth or your own abilities as a writer?

3. Are you continuing to work on a project out of fear of letting it go? Why are you afraid?

4. Do you fritter away some of your writing time by thinking about the fate of a current project, such as whether or not it will be published?

5. Do you find yourself talking about ideas before putting anything on paper, only to find you have talked away your interest in, and energy for, the project itself?

Put It On Paper

PROMPT: If you have an idea you've been carrying around in your mind for a while, stop reading this book and put something on paper. Even if you can only spend five minutes doing it, spend the five minutes. If you're hesitant to begin writing, just describe the story in a paragraph or write five possible titles or name all the characters. But do it now. This very minute. Seriously. I'm not kidding. Go. You shouldn't be reading this sentence, unless you've taken time to do this prompt.

PROMPT: Write about your idea as if you're telling it to someone, a good friend or someone who is supportive of you. You may want to conjure an ideal reader. Tell the story from beginning to end. Avoid telling any background for the idea, such as how you thought of it or how it relates to your life. Just focus on the story itself.

PROMPT: No doubt you have read something and said, "What a great idea." Write a list of these pieces of writing. You may need to brainstorm a bit to recall them. You may want to keep a running list, adding to it as you recall more pieces. Try to detect any patterns in your list, any elements shared by some of the entries. Does your list contain, for example, a lot of romantic comedies? Stories of the West? Stories about parents and parenthood? Do you seem to be drawn to biographies? Thrillers? Lyric poems? This type of list can provide a perspective on your tastes as a writer and can steer you toward subjects and forms to which you instinctively respond.

PROMPT: Write a pledge to yourself to keep secret an idea for a writing project. Tell no one about it. If you tend to be a blabbermouth, as we writers often are, give the pact with yourself a time limit, such as: "I'll keep this idea a secret for one month, during which I'll write a little something on it every day."

PROMPT: Write about the praise you've received for your writing, whether from a high school English teacher or an editor or a friend. If you want, list as many as you can remember. Keep this list handy. When doubts arise while working on an idea, take out your list and descriptions and read them quickly. All writers need such affirmations.

PROMPT: In a few paragraphs evaluate the project you're questioning. What are its strengths and weaknesses? What will you need to accomplish on the page to bring the project to the level you hope to achieve with it? Imagine what you would be doing if you did not have the project, if you put it aside or, perhaps, it never existed at all. If the project seems flat to you now, examine the possible reasons for that feeling. Have you worked it so long that the energy is gone? Does it explore a subject or a situation that is no longer meaningful to you? If the project is of a personal nature, consider whether you're avoiding some key aspect of the story that you don't want to explore. Consider your reasons for avoiding that part of the story.

PROMPT: In a few paragraphs, assess yourself as a writer—your strengths and weaknesses. Which elements of the craft have you mastered? Which ones do you hope to master? What do you enjoy most about writing? What do you find most frustrating? What needs does it serve? What pleasures does it bring? What sacrifices does it require? In another paragraph or two, write what your life would be like without writing. What would change about you and about how you spend your time?

PROMPT: Spend a writing session recalling on paper how you came to an idea and developed it in the past. What inspired the idea? How did it take hold in your mind? What steps did you take to bring the idea to life on paper? If you've completed a number of projects in the past, write about the process of developing them. Can you find patterns in the way you've worked, and succeeded, in the past? Understanding the way you work will help you in developing future ideas.

PROMPT: If you have an idea but doubt your ability to develop and complete it successfully, imagine that you're the greatest writer in the history of literature. How would such a writer develop it? What moves would he or she make? Spend a session exploring the idea from this writer's perspective.

PROMPT: If you've been working on a piece for a good while and feel it may be time to let go, to put it away for a while, give yourself a deadline for working on it. For example, tell yourself you'll spend the next five sessions on the piece before putting it away. Then, stick to that schedule, even if the piece suddenly comes to life. If it does come to life, you can bring it out again later but for now you've decided to move on to something new.

Chapter Two

A World of Ideas

Let's agree on something right from the start: The ideas you seek, the ones that you'll use to write beautiful work, are already inside you. They're in your memory and your subconscious. Those that are in the world around you exist only as they connect with your imagination. They can flower into life only through what you bring to them. Too often I see writers flailing about in search of The Great Idea that will sweep them to success. When they hear of a book or film or poem that succeeds, they chide themselves for not having thought of the idea first. Then they strain even harder to find The Great Idea. They strive so hard to be "creative" that they miss what is in front of them.

A cod was just a simple, stupid fish, but it spoke in some way to the mind and imagination of Mark Kurlansky, who used it to give readers a new way of looking at the history of the western world in his book *Cod*. Carol Shields uses a seemingly outdated narrative device in *The Stone Diaries* to tell a character's life story, but she makes it seem fresh, even somewhat experimental. The whole of Nicholson Baker's novel *The Mezzanine* involves a man buying shoelaces during his lunch break. The film *My Dinner with Andre* consists entirely of a single long dinner conversation between two characters. And so, once again, it's not the idea; it's what you do with it.

In his book titled *Creativity, Unleashing the Forces Within*, Osho, a spiritual teacher, makes the following statement about relaxation:

I have never seen a person who has become relaxed through reading a book about relaxation. He has become more hectic, because now his whole life of activity remains untouched, his obsession is there to be active, the disease is there, and he pretends to be in a relaxed state.

This insight also applies to creativity. No book will give you the magic key to unlock your creativity. Only by being receptive to yourself, to the mythology of your own mind, will you find The Great Ideas that exist inside you already. Explore what's there and allow yourself to respond instinctively to the ideas that well up. In this chapter, we'll look at some ways to explore, aspects of yourself and the world that can lead you to the creative part of yourself.

The Secret of Creative Genius

As we launch into the methods for generating ideas and, later, for developing them, let me state the obvious: if you don't put your responses to the prompts on paper, you won't get your money's worth from this book. You won't build a storehouse of ideas. So create a computer file for your responses, or dedicate a notebook or reserve a section in a notebook you've already begun. *But you must write.* Like learning any craft or sport or activity, it's a two-part process. You are taught a process, and then you must do the process. You need to practice a process to learn it.

I've had the pleasure of working for some time with Doug Hall, a creativity specialist who develops methods mostly for businesses. He teaches individuals as well as enormous corporations how to generate profitable ideas. *Inc.* magazine once called him "America's #1 Idea Man." Doug has a theory he calls "a million times zero equals zero." He means that a person can create a million ideas or can create an idea that's worth a million dollars, but if steps aren't taken to implement the idea, it's worth nothing. It generates zero sales. He writes books about business creativity and presents lectures and seminars across the country, and those who hear or read his message usually are fired with inspiration. Many, however, do nothing with their inspiration. And so their million-dollar ideas earn no money at all.

The same is true for books on writing. I hear writers and critics decry such books, proclaiming that no one ever learned to write from reading a book about it. In fact, I have read many excellent books on writing and have learned much from them. I feel any serious writer should be familiar with at least a few books on the craft. However, the books can only take us so far. The rest of the learning process takes place during the writing itself. We can think of dozens of ideas for stories and novels and screenplays and essays and so on, but if we don't put them on paper and take the time to push them a bit, we will have nothing to show for our creativity.

As you wend your way through this book, take time to do some of the prompts. Honor your written responses to the prompts by keeping them in some fashion. Some will lead you to fully developed projects. Others won't. But like Doug Hall's disciples, you can end up with a million or with zero. You have the power to choose which you'd prefer to have.

I've taken a final piece of advice on this subject from another creativity guru, Andrei Aleinikov, whose book *MegaCreativity: 5 Steps to Thinking Like a Genius* offers many wonderful approaches to generating ideas. Here's an exercise from the book that I particularly like:

1. Choose a word at random. Any word. The first one that comes into your mind. Open a dictionary and let your finger fall on a word. If you're in a group, have each person tell the other person a word. Write down the word.
2. Write down a type of flower: orchid, rose, violet, whatever.
3. Write down a human quality that you particularly admire, such as courage or humility or intelligence.
4. Now write three sentences using all three words in each sentence. And this is a timed exercise. You have three minutes. Go.

Finished? Did you write the three sentences? I'll bet you didn't need the full three minutes, right? Did you use that time to write a fourth sentence? A fifth?

Probably not. And that is the real meaning of the exercise. We are trained to follow orders, even in matters involving creativity. A person in authority tells us to write *three* sentences, and so we write three of them. When you read the paragraphs opening this chapter, you probably thought the points were pretty obvious. "Sure, sure, the ideas are already inside me. I know that. And the Indian guy is right about books telling us how to relax, and, yep, I agree about the same holding true for creativity." And yet, we quickly disregard what we know, because the business about the three sentences and three types of words has a certain magic formula quality about it. I felt the same way when I attended a lecture given by Dr. Aleinikov. When I conduct creativity workshops at writers conferences, I sometimes use this exercise, and there's usually a collective groan when "the trick" is revealed. We feel disappointed. We hoped we had stumbled upon the magic formula, even when, if someone had told us there are no magic formulas, we'd have said, "Of course. That's so obvious."

The second lesson of the exercise is that creativity is linked with work. The writers who succeeded at the exercise are those who wrote more than was asked of them. They pushed beyond the limits of the exercise. They worked harder. Now, you might be a creative genius, and stories just flow easily through your fingers and onto the keys and onto the page. If so, you can stop reading. You have no need for this book. But if you're like nearly all writers, you've learned that sometimes writing is tough, and the ideas, like a stubborn pet, don't come when they're called. We have to work. We have to generate a lot of writing to generate good writing. If other writers are writing three sentences, be willing to write five sentences. Work harder. And when you do, they'll say you're a creative genius, and they'll believe that ideas just come a lot easier to you than they do to them.

After one of my workshops at a bookstore, I was approached by a woman who had raised her hand when I asked how many people had written more than three sentences. She'd written six sentences, more than anyone else, and by doing so she won a decorated bookmark. She admitted in a somewhat guilty, sheepish tone that the only reason she'd written more than three was because the first three she wrote "were so bad." She told me, "I had to keep trying until I got one that wasn't terrible." She felt she'd won the award unfairly. "If I were as good a writer as some of the others I wouldn't have had to write so many." She even wanted to give back the bookmark. But, for reasons I needn't explain to you, her statement was the perfect embodiment of the exercise's goal. She wasn't satisfied with her first three sentences so she kept trying. As you respond to the prompts in this chapter and throughout the book, as you develop your ideas, your works won't always align themselves into brilliant, inspired sentences. When that happens, don't berate yourself. Keep trying.

The Road to Discovery

As we agreed at the beginning of the chapter, the process of getting ideas for writing is one of discovery. The ideas we use for writing already exist within our imaginations, waiting to be found and developed. Many lay within our memories, our thoughts and feelings. We remember the look on a brother's face as he headed off to college. We remember the smell of fresh oranges in a hotel lobby on a family vacation we took many years ago. We have always believed in the power of prayer or in the value of honesty. Fall is our favorite season. There is a moment or two in our lives in which, to quote Scott Fitzgerald, "life was a dream." We return to a certain novel every few years, one we've read a half dozen times already, and every time we fall under its spell. A friend's comment made ten years ago still makes us laugh. A steaming bowl of clam chowder on a snowy winter's day is one of the great pleasures in life.

Our memories, like Whitman's poem, "contain multitudes." Begin the process of generating ideas by exploring these multitudes. Search your memory for images and events, for people and places that possess a certain power for you, ones that elicit a strong reaction. Use whatever method you prefer to brainstorm ideas to help you or simply make lists while brainstorming. In all cases, don't censor anything at this stage. Even if the memory is goofy or if you have no idea why you still remember something because it has no resonance for you anymore.

When you begin writing about any of the items on your list, try to avoid the "My Most Embarrassing Moment" approach often used in high school writing classes. That assignment can be fruitful in a class setting with students who are not interested in writing. It directs them to write about a subject they feel strongly about. But for you, it can be limiting. It plops you into a frame of reference (and of writing) that is familiar and often mechanical. It also limits your imagination to *the* one moment of embarrassment or happiness or whatever. You're going deeper. You're open to less apocalyptic moments. And you're open to ones that possess more subtlety. You're open to ones you don't understand. And you're open to images, to fragments of event and conversation, sensory details unrelated to any event you can recall.

Reaching Out

Exploring the landscape of memory, as surely you discovered in the previous section, could provide a lifetime's worth of writing projects. But perhaps you prefer to write about the world outside you. As far as exploring painful personal moments goes, you've been there, done that, bought the hair shirt, and moved on. In that case, while the rest of us neurotic writers envy the hell out of you, you're free to brainstorm about issues and ideas that interest you. Ones that rouse your passion and energy. Current events or historical ones. Your opinion on everything from stem cell research to the Bay of Pigs. Brainstorm lists or create clusters or use any other method that works for you. Get your ideas on paper. Explore the ones with which you most intensely connect. As we discussed earlier, the idea exists in its connection to your imagination and your passion. For you, the subject of endangered timber wolves in the Yukon is loaded with a book's worth of ideas. For someone else, it's a worthy cause and even one they would be interested in reading about, but it's not grist for their literary mill.

A caveat: Some writers focus on issues of national interest because they want their writing to seem topical. They also fear that writing about themselves won't interest readers. Some even hope to capitalize on a trend by writing about this or that subject. And some write about impersonal issues because personal ones are too frightening. At this stage of the process, don't censor any ideas, but do keep in mind that if a subject—even a personal one—is interesting to you, it's possible to make it interesting to others. Writing about topical subjects in order to catch trends or because you believe there's a large audience interested in the subject, though you're not particularly interested yourself, can lead to flat, dull pieces. They lack the true engagement of the writer.

At the same time, if you write only about personal experiences and feelings, consider broadening your range. Is there a way to link your personal experience to a larger issue? For example, I wrote a piece for a magazine about the wave of Catholic priests who had been accused of sexual misconduct with students. The issue was on the news every night at that time. Several priests from my high school, ones who had been teachers of mine, made local news as part of this wave. In the piece, I fused the national story with the local one and added my own experience in going back to the high school after so many years. The national issue, the local news angle, and the personal reflections combined to make the piece more powerful than any one of those elements would have allowed it to be.

To combine the strengths of a personal connection with the scope of a well-known event or person, pull an item or two from each of your lists and look for ways to bring them together into a single piece of writing. Try to find the personal connection in the public. Try to find the public connection in the personal.

A Place You've Never Been

Some writers eschew the personal as well as the public, at least on the surface of their work. They work entirely in made-up worlds. The most obvious form of this type of writing is fantasy and science fiction, in which worlds are completely made up. But I also refer to all types of fiction—from short stories and novels to plays and screenplays—that do not seem to be grounded in the author's experience in any way. The central conflict has nothing to do with anything that ever happened to the author or anything the author has read or heard about. The characters are totally fabricated.

Of course, we can plunge at this point into the familiar discussion about whether or not we're able to make up such stories, that even if the story didn't happen to us or to anyone we know, it must be grounded in some way in our experience. The tale of a man's escape from a penal colony on Neptune in the year 2510 connects at some level with the writer, who perhaps is being pursued by an ex-spouse or the IRS (certainly more daunting foes than a bunch of irate Neptunians). But let's not pursue this angle. Some writers think and write in this way, following the lead of their imaginations. They come up with a situation that engages them or the voice of a character begins speaking to them on paper. If you are this type of writer—or even if you're not—take time now to explore characters and conflicts that have resonated for you in the past. Focus, perhaps, on stories that you've thought about writing but never did, ones that return again and again. Consider stories that you've tried to write but those of which you've managed to create only fragments. Make a list or a cluster of these stories—their titles or a brief description or even something as simple as "the Fiona story" or "story where guy wrecks his fishing boat near the Keys."

If you aren't by nature compelled to write such invented tales, try creating your alternate reality. If your job is dull and predictable, sketch a scenario in which a woman battles all sorts of pressures and conflicts at work. If you've not traveled much in your life, write about a peripatetic person. Playwright Eugene O'Neill used this approach to write *Ah, Wilderness*, his only comedy. As you know, O'Neill tended to write plays full of despair and anguish. His best known play, *A Long Day's Journey into Night*, is an autobiographical examination of his family. Mother, father and two sons snarl and rage and lie to each other during a single day in their lives. In

Ah, Wilderness he wrote about the family he wanted to have, his d\
family. That family, the Millers, live in a small Connecticut town, as do\
Tyrones in *Journey*. In fact, the plays have a number of parallels, even
some similar lines of dialogue. Give this approach a try.

The prompts that follow offer a number of specific ways for exploring
your inner and outer worlds as well as worlds sprung completely from
your imagination. There is no *right* approach, so experiment with all of
them. Look for ways to combine them. When one of them sparks an idea
you want to explore at length, keep moving. Push beyond the limits of
the prompt. Be the writer who writes six sentences when only three are
required.

Questions to Consider

1. Do you sense creative powers inside you that you can't seem
   to reach? How might you reach them?
2. At some level of your mind are you looking for the Magic
   Formula of Creativity? We may pshaw such formulas, but
   our search can continue even if we don't admit it to ourselves. Is this true for you?
3. Do you write mostly about personal experience, about public issues and events, or about invented characters and situations? If you don't write much at all, which of the three
   draws you most?
4. Which of the three approaches we've discussed is closest
   to the type of writing you like to read? Does this match what
   you like to write?

Put It On Paper

 PROMPT: Make a list of your top ten all-time most important memories,
good or bad. Focus on the life-changing ones, experiences that made a
difference in your life. Choose one or two and explore it in a page or two.

If you want, make a list of "Most" memories. Most wonderful, shameful, embarrassing, guilt-inducing, peaceful, etc. Choose one and write a couple of pages or so about it. As I mentioned earlier in the chapter, sometimes these "Most" moments are less fruitful than less significant ones, but take time to explore them a bit. Then, move to less obvious ones. Trust your instincts as you brainstorm this list. You might think at first that the moment wasn't important, wasn't life-changing or in any way significant. Never mind these censoring devices. What moments well up when considered in this context? Write them down. Then choose a few to explore at greater length. This type of moment can be more fun to write about than the big ones, because you've thought about it less and it doesn't come with a prearranged meaning. And yet, when making a list of moments, it occurred to you, so surely it's important in some way. You need to discover its importance.

PROMPT: Write about a place you've never been, one in which you've always had an interest or somewhere that inspired a feeling of connection. Investigate your interest or connection.

PROMPT: Write "Images from My Life" at the top of a page. In a timed brainstorm session (shoot for five or ten minutes), write down the images that come to mind. Relax and yield your mind to the task. Don't try to force any mental pictures or focus on what you consider the key images of your life. Allow the images themselves to well naturally from your mind. Circle one and explore it on paper, writing down the who, when, why, where, and how. You can repeat this process several times and still arrive at many useful images. Sometimes the second or third batches are more fruitful than the first, because they're ones you remember less frequently. You haven't given them such a clear meaning or context yet.

PROMPT: Use the same process as we used in the previous prompt, but focus on other general categories, such as places or people. Circle the one that most engages you and explore at length. To help you explore even further, when you write about people, try to find a moment—something they did or said that epitomizes them in some way. With places, try to find a detail or an event that epitomizes your experience with, or your sense of, the place.

PROMPT: Here's your writing schedule for the week. Write one page per day, reacting to the subject in whatever way you want. The titles are from novels, stories, and essays, and I've chosen less known ones by intention. If you recognize any of them, find a different one to use, perhaps the chapter title of a book you haven't read. If you miss a day, just carry over the subject to the next day. Monday: Why I'm a Danger to the Public. Tuesday: Love Letters. Wednesday: A Gracious Rain. Thursday: Gas Stations. Friday: Lullaby. Saturday: The Right Thing to Do at the Time. Sunday: Cloud. These titles can spark a fictional story or a piece of nonfiction, a personal reflection, or a SF novel. You can create a schedule yourself, of course. Whip through a half-dozen anthologies on your bookshelves and pull some titles at random. Go for variety in length and tone to keep yourself from exploring only one type of writing. For yet another variation, thumb through anthologies and steal first sentences.

PROMPT: Let's use the same week-long approach but broaden the subjects. The only rule is that you aren't allowed to write the same type of piece two days in a row. For example, if you respond to Monday's prompt with a piece of personal reflection, you must respond on Tuesday with a piece of fiction or a piece with a more public bent. Here we go: Monday: Revenge. Tuesday: A Family Gathering. Wednesday: Playing Favorites. Thursday: Fear. Friday: The Love of My life. Saturday: The Solution. Sunday: Dignity.

PROMPT: Here's another week's worth of prompts, though this one asks you to explore a single subject in greater depth. Choose a subject from one of the previous prompts, perhaps one you've already responded to in writing or any one that especially appeals to you. For example, let's choose

"A Family Gathering." Monday: Write a personal reflection. You might write about a gathering of your own family such as at an event or during a holiday. Tuesday: Begin a piece of fiction based on Monday's reflection. For the family gathering, fictionalize the event, adding details or creating an imagined conflict (or heightening a real one). Wednesday: Find a picture in a book or magazine or on the Internet that portrays your subject. Write about it in whatever way that engages you. For a family gathering, you could compare the pictured family to your own or write a more general essay on the nature of family. Or you could begin a short story using the moment frozen in the photograph as your beginning. Thursday: Find a quote about your subject that speaks to you in some way. Use a quote book or flip through a magazine focused on the subject. Write an opinion piece responding to the quote. Friday: Write about your subject in a way that is opposite to your opinion or experience. For a family gathering, write about one that is completely different from your own. If your family is a bunch of drunken rowdies, for example, write about a very dignified gathering. Saturday: Review everything you've written for the week on your subject and write a few pages fusing elements from several (or all) of your pieces. You could have a character in your fictional family repeat the real-life quote you used on Thursday. Sunday: Pick one of the pieces from the week and push deeper into it, extending it by writing another page or two. Can you keep going?

P R O M P T : Let's mix approaches, combining the public and the private. Write a paragraph or two about a well-known event or issue. Now write a paragraph or two about some personal connection you have to this event or issue. You needn't be directly involved—any connection will do. For example, you could write about the war with Iraq, recounting the steps the government took to initiate the war, then write about your own feelings about the war or about a relative who was involved.

P R O M P T : Let's mix the ideas you created in previous prompts. Choose an item from your list of "most" experiences, then choose one from your "images" list. Spend a session fusing them, placing the image into a piece about the experience, even if they're completely unrelated in terms of your experience. In fact, make sure they're unrelated. The key is discovering and forging the relationship.

 PROMPT: Create a prompt of your own. One of the themes of this chapter is that creativity requires moving past what you've been told to do, and so what I'm telling you to do is tell yourself what to do. You might want to brainstorm a half-dozen "assignments" and choose one to explore in a session. The key here is to set forth your own task and then find ways to accomplish it.

Chapter Three

The Idea File

A struggling writer once told me, "It's not that I don't have any ideas, it's that I don't have any good ones. And when I do think of one I always forget it." She was being self-effacingly tongue-in-cheek, but her statement brings up two aspects of getting ideas. First, she judges her ideas too quickly, deciding, sometimes before a word hits the page, that they're not "good ones." Second, she forgets them. We all forget them from time to time. Sometimes they return to our memory, triggered by some comment or event. Other times, they're gone for good.

Thus, we must follow the age-old advice about keeping a notebook for writing down those ideas. Some writers disdain this advice, saying, "If an idea is any good, you'll remember it." I disagree. Many good ideas or potentially good ideas are lost because we neglect to give ourselves a reminder. Keeping a notebook is a great reminder. Some writers organize their notebooks into subject areas, such as "Story Ideas" and "Characters" and "Titles" and "Dialogue." When they need a character or a bit of dialogue, they know just where to go.

Others keep a more general notebook, scribbling thoughts and ideas anywhere in the notebook. Though this approach is more haphazard, it does preserve the idea. A few such writers have said that this approach works better for them, because it simplifies the process. If they had to flip to a particular section of the notebook and keep everything organized, they'd be less likely to do it on a regular basis. I must admit I'm among this group. I've tried the more organized approach and found I didn't stick to it. Also, rare was the time when I needed a good line of dialogue and flipped to the "Dialogue" section to find exactly what I needed. Instead, the notebook provided not only reminders of ideas that I would have forgotten, but a more general type of inspiration as well.

Some writers avoid categorizing their ideas, because they want to keep them fluid. A snippet of dialogue, for example, could also be a story idea or the basis for a character. They feel such codifying works against their creativity. Another reason for putting everything in one place is that it allows for interesting accidents. Seemingly unrelated ideas can spring to life through unintended juxtapositions.

A box of index cards can be used as an alternative to the notebook. Some writers prefer this method, which can be easier to manipulate than a notebook. The cards can be shuffled around, and it's easier to snatch one when inspiration strikes. To keep them organized by category, if that's your goal, you can use tabbed dividers that make it easy to flip to whichever category you want. I know of a few writers who use index cards but simply toss the cards into a box. From time to time, they'll sort through the box in search of a creative spark. The act of writing the idea down plants it more firmly in their memories, even if they never read the card again.

In recent years, I've kept a notebook, but I've relied more often on (and used more regularly) a system of file folders. When I see an article in the paper that interests me or offers an idea, I rip it out and stick it in a folder. When I think of a story idea or hear a stretch of dialogue in my mind, I write it down on whatever is handy—a napkin or the back of an envelope. Afterward, I'll put that in a folder. Some writers I know will copy these stray bits of writing into their notebooks. They say that when copying them into the notebook they sometimes expand or develop the idea. To them, I give a tip of the writer's beret. Their approach makes sense, and if you can use it, use it. But I know that if I was faced with having to copy an envelope's worth of description into my notebook, I'd probably not do it. We all must recognize our weaknesses. But if I need only shove the envelope into a file folder, I will do that.

I keep separate file folders for book and magazine ideas. I also have specific folders for types of ideas, such as "sports" or "history" or "pop culture." If an idea sticks around for a while and begins to develop into something, it is awarded a file of its own. Into these files go scribblings and clipped articles and pamphlets and appropriate Web addresses, book titles, anything that gives me a new idea or relates to one that's still percolating.

My point here is not to recommend my method but to devise a method that works for you, one that feels comfortable and is easy for you to access and to use. There's not a right or wrong way to collect and preserve your ideas. You may have a system in place already. And writers tend to refine and change their systems, so don't be afraid to do that.

Also, don't limit your idea file to stray thoughts you've recorded on paper. It can include an entire essay or a school report on a subject that remains interesting to you. It can include newspaper articles and matchbooks, photographs clipped from magazines, postcards, souvenirs. In short: anything you want.

A friend of mine was casting about for his next book idea when his agent called with one of his own. The agent had clipped a tiny article out of a newspaper a number of years before. The article concerned an unusual group of soldiers in World War II who spent much of the war creating diversions and deceptions. The group was made up of actors, painters, radio engineers, and sound-effects technicians. Very little had been written about them. By keeping the article, the agent never forgot the story and offered it to my friend, who researched the group and wrote a splendid book titled *Secret Soldiers*. A clipped article led to a published book.

Working the File

Stuffing things in a file folder or a desk drawer or writing them down in a notebook doesn't do a whole lot of good if you don't review your holdings from time to time. Some writers allocate specific times for reviewing their idea collections, such as once a month or every few weeks. I know a few writers who check once a week or before every writing session, especially when they don't have an on-going project. Some writers do an annual file purge, sifting through their files or notebooks and discarding ideas that no longer appeal to them or seem relevant.

I don't do this, because I'm afraid at some point the idea might have a fresh appeal or might strike me in a different way. The plethora of organization and de-clutter books on the bookstore shelves would find this a bad habit, perhaps even a weakness of character, a sign of an inability to let go of the past. If so, I stand guilty as charged.

Find a system of reviewing your ideas that works for you. You should review them often enough that you know what you have in the file, but I don't know that any other "rules" can be applied. As I mentioned earlier, you can use this time to look for connections between ideas. Or you might find that an idea in the file, even one written some time ago, connects with the project you're currently developing. If so, explore the connection.

Reviewing your idea file from time to time also can give you a shot of confidence by providing evidence that you're a creative person. Here is proof that you've awakened in the middle of the night so taken by a thought that you had to write it down. You've honed your powers of observation to the point where you've noticed, and recorded, your impressions of an event or a person. You've described a place or written a scene or put together a few stanzas of poetry. When you're feeling that you never have good ideas, like the friend I mentioned at the beginning of the chapter, you can prove to yourself that you have plenty of them. Finally, reviewing your idea file on a regular basis will make you want to add to it. The process has the effect of triggering new ideas and reminding you of ones you've forgotten. I can't explain that phenomenon, but I've experienced it many times.

Collecting your ideas into a notebook or a file or even a cardboard box can spark your next project. They also can bring new life and energy to an on-going project. As we work our way through this book, add to your file or notebook. Keep it growing. Most of all, collecting your ideas and preserving them honors those ideas. By its existence it says that these contents are valuable, these thoughts and writings and ideas sprang from your imagination and connected with you in some way. And they can lead to something wonderful.

Questions to Consider

1. Do you save your ideas for writing in some manner? If not, why not? If so, is it working for you. Is there a better method to use?

2. What are the best writing ideas you've ever had? Is there a connection between them? Have any been forgotten, been only partially developed or remained dormant? Is it time to pursue them?

3. How well do you take care of your ideas? Do you toss them off and forget about them? Do you judge and discard them quickly?

4. How do you usually respond to other people's ideas? Do you show enthusiasm and offer encouragement, or do you more often find fault? Are you threatened by the ideas, feeling that you should have thought of that first or wondering why other people have better ideas than you do? Compare your responses to questions three and four. People often find they're more generous toward others' ideas than they are to their own.

Put It On Paper

PROMPT: You've probably had many ideas for writing that you've never written down. Here's your chance to do it. Brainstorm as many as you can recall. You might even want to write "Ideas" in a circle and create a "web" or "cluster" of thoughts around it.

PROMPT: Pick one of the ideas you generated in the previous prompt. Don't think much about it. Which one comes first to mind? Then, spend some time exploring and developing that idea. If it's a snippet of dia-

logue, for example, expand it into a full scene. If it's nothing r
a title, write the first three paragraphs of a piece that the title _____ ___.

PROMPT: Thinking like a writer, respond in a paragraph to each of the
following words. What thoughts for writing does each word spark? You
might want to develop a single idea or write down a batch of them for
later development.

Family	Surprises
Adventure	Intensity
Faith	Place
Transition	Leaving
Love	Health
Oddballs	

After finishing your responses to these words, you may want to make a
list of your own. Brainstorm a short list, writing whatever words come
quickly to mind, then respond.

PROMPT: Sift through some ideas you've been brewing for a while. If
you haven't written them down in a notebook or placed them in some
type of file, do that first. Look for interesting juxtapositions. That line
you overheard at a restaurant might connect with the next note, the one
about a story involving your trip to Greece.

PROMPT: Try a more conscious and direct approach to the previous
prompt. Pluck three ideas from your file and write a short piece using
all three. What connections can you create?

PROMPT: If one of those de-clutter nazis came to your home and told
you that you could keep only three ideas in your collection (as a way of
reducing your emotional baggage and lightening your spiritual load, of
course), which ones would you keep? Spend some time developing each
of those ideas.

PROMPT: Spend some time with your junk—your souvenirs and trinkets, old gifts and holiday cards, broken toys and photographs. All the stuff that for one reason or another you haven't thrown out or given away. Write a short piece—even just a paragraph—about each item or choose the ones that interest you most. You could focus on how you came to have it, the people involved in your having it, or simply how it makes you feel now. Put the pieces you write in your idea file.

PROMPT: Spend a few moments with your music. Choose a half-dozen or so tapes or CDs—or records, if you still have them—and play them. Listen to them alone and jot down your thoughts. Listening to music is a wonderful way to trigger memories, and it can bring back thoughts and feelings from long ago. You might write about the feelings each piece of music evokes or about the memories. You might write about the tape or CD itself, such as when you bought it and why, what it means to you, why it remains part of your collection.

PROMPT: Some memories never lose their power. For example, we feel as embarrassed now as we were then about something we did in high school. Or that shrew/jerk who dumped us years ago still makes our lips curl and blood boil. Have you written about these times and these feelings? They're hanging around for a reason. Give one a try.

Chapter Four

The Water's Fine

So let's jump in. With luck, you're already in, splashing around, whizzing a floppy Frisbee at fellow swimmers. To ditch the metaphor: You have a writing project underway. You might have responded to a prompt in one of the earlier chapters and are moving forward. If not, you've created some type of idea file and can pluck a favorite from it and begin writing. If you've not yet created a file and you're not sure what to write about, let's consider a few options.

Return to chapter two and pick one of the prompts. Several prompts offer at least seven idea-sparkers. You could choose one of them. Or you could select a prompt at the end of this chapter or from a chapter further on in the book, though most of those will focus on adding ideas to an existing idea. If you want even more possibilities, a number of books offer them. First, please indulge a plug for my own *The Writer's Idea Book*. I also wrote most of the prompts in a book published some years ago titled *Idea Catcher: An Inspiring Journal for Writers*. Monica Wood's *The Pocket Muse: Ideas and Inspirations for Writing* is another source of prompts, as is *What If? Writing Exercises for Fiction Writers* by Anne Bernays and Pam Painter. With the proliferation of Web sites for writers, the Internet is packed with prompts. Use one of these sources if you're looking for ways to get started on a project.

When you have a project in motion, even if you've only written a few paragraphs, take some time to focus on it. At this stage, we're just playing. Don't put pressure on yourself or judge the project as good or bad. You don't know what it is yet, so there's no point in trying to determine if it's any good. You might be right in the middle, so don't spend hours trying to write a perfect first sentence. That's way too much for now. You're a kid, playing in a mud puddle. Swirl the water with your finger, and watch the dirt roil from the bottom. Jab a finger down deep and feel the tug of suction as you pull the finger out. Splash around. Play.

I'm not being intentionally vague or poetic here. At this stage of the process, it's tough to offer much in the way of specific guidance. You're discovering an idea, following it intuitively, waiting for characters to assert themselves, a conflict to reveal itself, a shape to begin to form, a voice to rise from the page. Allow these things to happen, but try not to force them. The key, for now, is opening yourself to possibilities. At this stage, the piece is quite fragile. It requires a gentle touch. It also requires attention. When a piece is getting underway, return to it often—everyday, if possible. If you leave it for too long, you risk losing inspiration for it. The magic of the piece disappears because you can no longer feel its rhythms as intuitively as when you return to it frequently.

Techniques for Exploring

There are many ways to explore an idea when it's beginning to form. None is more right than another. Through experience, you'll find what works for you. One way is to approach it from a variety of angles, as we did in the prompt in chapter two involving "A Family Gathering." We wrote personal reflections about the subject, and we wrote opinion pieces. We wrote about it as fiction. We looked for relevant quotes and photographs and responded to them. We tried to fuse these approaches into a single piece. This approach keeps us open to possibilities.

Allow the point of view to shift. Allow characters' names to change. If you want to write a reportorial or academic piece but personal stories keep creeping in, let them. If you're writing a memoir of a childhood incident, allow yourself to shift from your adult perspective to a present tense account. In fact, play with that shift, moving back and forth until one establishes itself. If you're writing a screenplay, capture lines of dialogue in whatever order they come. Don't pour your story into the three-act formula before developing its possibilities outside that formula.

Sometimes we get bogged down at the start because we're not sure where to start. We have a sense of the story, but we're not sure where to begin. If you've just begun putting it on paper, start anywhere. Get something on paper. Pundits tell us to start as close to the end as possible, and that's good advice, once you know the ending. For now, allow yourself to move around. And if you're too sure of the ending, you may be stalled by the fact that the story is already neatly resolved in your mind. It feels stale from the start. If that's the case, start with a new ending. Begin by writing your ending or conclusion in a fresh way.

Like many writers, I try to focus on characters at this stage, when I'm writing fiction. Usually my idea for a piece begins with a character or two. I follow them to their jobs, try to figure out where they live, try to get into their heads for a while. When I move too quickly to The Story, they sometimes are swallowed by it, becoming what I call Plot Pawns rather than fully realized characters. Some fiction writers, however, move first to the situation. The energy of a conflict drives the early stages of the story, and characters are discovered and developed as the plot unfolds.

For personal essays and memoirs, the early stages of a project can be fraught with self-consciousness. We think: Who cares what happened to me? We wonder if the personal story and ideas we're relating are of any interest to readers who don't know us. Trusting your impulse to write the piece is crucial. Delay the judge. Or agree that the whole thing is silly and self-indulgent, but you're going to do it anyway rather than plop in front of the television. The other concern is what to put in and what to leave out. If you're being completely open and not censoring, how do you know which details about an event or situation to include? The fact is, you don't. That's why early drafts of memoirs tend to seem unfocused. One memory leads to another, and before you know it you're off on a tangent. Later in this book, we'll discuss ways of deciding between important details and extraneous ones. For now, put in whatever relates to the idea you're developing.

In his book *Lessons from a Lifetime of Writing*, David Morrell explains his method of interviewing himself in order to explore a new idea. When beginning a novel, he writes extended question-and-answer interviews with himself to better understand the nature, scope, and possibilities of an idea and his interest in it. He asks basic questions about the characters or about the reasons behind his inspiration. His responses to the questions allow him to write down his thoughts without the framework of chapters and opening lines and so on. At some point, a response to a question grows into the novel itself, and he's underway.

In *Writing the Blockbuster Novel*, Al Zuckerman explains how Ken Follett, a very successful client of Zuckerman's literary agency, develops a series of heavily annotated outlines for a novel before he begins writing it in earnest. The outlines can be changed while the writing is in progress, but mostly he sticks close to them. Some writers would find such a method confining. Others couldn't live without it.

In the late 1980s and early 1990s, literary disciples of renowned editor Gordon Lish focused on finding the first sentence of a story. They believed the rest of the story would flow naturally from it. This approach was successful with a certain type of literary short story, but most writers would never complete a single project if they had to hone a perfect first sentence before moving on. I had a friend in graduate school who would think about an idea for weeks before writing it. Then he would revise and revise the first page over and over. As poor graduate students in the early 1980s, we didn't have computers. I remember seeing more than a dozen typed versions of that first page on his sawhorse desk.

Some writers need to carry an idea around in their heads for a while or doodle it on the page, knocking it around a bit, before it comes pouring out. You'll find what works for you, and maybe you've found the approach already. The key is finding a way of gently guiding a piece through its infancy, nudging it along in the direction it seems to want to take, and remaining open to shifts in direction.

At this stage, make a deal with yourself: You'll explore the idea for a specific number of pages before abandoning it. Give it a chance to grow. If you're a runner, you probably know that feeling of being tight and tired early in a run. A friend of mine calls it "feeling junky." Your breath is short and your legs are leaden. You think you'll never make your full course today. Ya just ain't got it today. But usually you find that if you keep running, you'll break through the junkiness and have yourself a good run. The same is true for writing. The going can be a little tough at first, but stay with it. Don't give up on a piece before it's had enough time to establish itself.

Questions to Consider

1. For now, don't ask questions. Write.

Put It On Paper

PROMPT: Choose one idea from your file or notebook. It need not even be your favorite. Write the first page or, if you have it pretty well underway, write the next page. At your next writing session, circle the phrase or detail or action that engages you most. Rather than continuing from where you stopped at the previous session, begin with what you've circled and write a new page.

PROMPT: After a writing session, write a congratulatory note from your ideal reader to you. The reader should tell you he or she loves your idea.

PROMPT: When your project is underway—at least a few pages on paper—write several paragraphs from a new point of view. If you're writing fiction, change the focal character. If you're writing an essay, change your authorial stance.

———

PROMPT: When you're in the first stage of a new project, write something on it every day for a week, even if you can only spare five or ten minutes. Touch base with it.

———

PROMPT: If you know what you want to write about but aren't sure where to start, begin with a line of dialogue, something you know is going to be said at some point in your piece. Write that line of dialogue and follow it, developing a single scene.

———

PROMPT: If you're stalled at the start, write at least a page from an omniscient point of view, in the god-like voices of nineteenth century novelists. Introduce the reader to your setting and situation, to the characters. For examples, check out Charles Dickens, Jane Austen, or William Makepeace Thackeray. You'll probably ditch that voice later, but for now use it to usher you in the story.

———

PROMPT: Still don't know where to start? Begin with the moment or detail or image that excites you most. Ignore that old rule about not getting your dessert until you eat your dinner. Start with dessert. For example: You want to write an essay about the break up of your romantic relationship, but you keep getting strangled by the endless details of backstory. Jump right to the climax. Give us the moment when somebody said he or she wants to leave. Develop it fully. Assume you'll do the explaining later.

———

PROMPT: If you're stalled at the start, shift to a different form. For example, if you're trying to write the break-up essay but after a page or two you're feeling like you're completely off the mark, shift to fiction for a session or two. Write it as a short story. Or you could shift perspective. Rather than telling it from the perspective of rueful-but-wiser you, the more innocent victim of the break-up, tell it from the perspective of the other person.

PROMPT: When you're stuck where to start or where to go next, write a general statement about the subject. For the break-up story, write a statement about the nature of break-ups. Then move to specific examples to show that what you've said is true. You could use these statements as section heads. Allow yourself to move away from the particulars of the break-up you were trying to write about.

PROMPT: If you have an idea and know where to begin but find yourself struggling with the first couple of paragraphs, skip them. Start on page two. Assume you've written those opening paragraphs and simply continue. We sometimes block ourselves by trying to perfect our openings, and sometimes we never get beyond that opening. Allow yourself to leap over it and get the story moving. You can go back later and create that wonderful opening sentence or paragraph that for the moment eludes you.

Chapter Five

Suspended Disbelief and Other Acts of Faith

There are many parallels between writing and falling in love. The process has a similar arc and similar obstacles. They have similar highs and lows and require similar resources from those who are successful.

Falling in love, for example, is the easy part. Finding someone to fall in love *with* can be tough, but when you find that someone, things usually launch onto a natural course. Life takes on a glow. There's a new zap of energy in the air and in everything around us. Ah, love's first tender bud. It's truly a remarkable thing.

I compare the initial "idea" stage of a project to the feeling of first falling in love. We may have to sort through some ideas, and we may find that one or two don't quite work or whose brief glimmer fades quickly. But when a good one hits, it feels great. And just like the first spark of romance, *getting* ideas is the easy part. It's also the most thrilling part, in some ways even the most fun. There's the high of inspiration, the glorious sense that the cares and strictures of the world have fallen away or at least been pushed into their proper perspective. We feel invulnerable. We feel perfectly connected to the natural order of life. We are who we are destined to be.

Then things get a little rocky.

In love, we suddenly realize that our partner is not perfect in every way: Must she be right about *everything*? Is he planning on coming over *every* night? You may even have a spat or two. And what the heck is this relationship anyway? What are we doing? Are we in love? Are we moving toward a deep commitment? Do we both want the same things?

In writing, after the first glow of idea-hood, even as we're humming along into chapter two or scene three, we begin to suspect that this story or essay or script isn't as perfect as we'd hoped. Looked at in a certain light, it's actually kind of stupid. Or pretentious. Or dull and obvious. Or maybe it's okay but certainly not the stroke of genius it seemed to be last week.

Many apprentice writers give up on the piece when they hit this first turn. It goes *bang* into the file cabinet, or worse, the trash basket. Alas, another failed idea. When oh when will the Right Idea come along? The answer is that, in fact, it might already have arrived. What's required is a renewed sense of involvement, an energy that we must create ourselves, because the first glow of inspiration has passed. Now things will get more complicated, will demand insight and compromise, will demand a certain level of blind faith.

Ron Carlson, well-known fiction writer and teacher, offers some advice about this stage of the process. He says that when we reach a point where the next step appears difficult, we get restless. We squirm in our chairs. Some writers will go get a fresh cup of coffee. Some will dive into household chores or catch up on e-mails or cut the grass. Others will stay in the chair and push forward. His advice is simple: "Be the writer who stays in the chair." I have that quote taped to an imaginary wall in my mind. When I find myself fidgeting because the first rush is over or some new scene or moment challenges me, maybe I don't know what comes next or I am having trouble making a sentence work, I repeat Carlson's advice aloud:

Be the writer who stays in the chair.

Whether you're struggling on one particular day or you're entering a new and difficult phase of a project that's been soaring along for weeks, you need to stay in the chair, sometimes literally, sometimes figuratively. As we move through the stages of a project we'll find many occasions for throwing up our hands and surrendering. But these stages truly are part of the process, just as working through differences is part of the process of building a relationship. They grow naturally out of your engagement with the material. In fact, they're *signs* of your engagement with the material.

That's Not Writer's Block. That's Writing.

If you bail out of the chair, you'll never know what might have happened had you faced the moment of consternation. Be the writer who stays in the chair. When you struggle to find the answers to the tricky questions posed by your story, when you push through the feeling that the piece is no longer as inspired or wonderful as it seemed at first blush, you push your project to its next level. And you push yourself forward as a writer. These are the victories that give us confidence, that make us brave enough to face the next set of difficulties.

I had the good fortune to hear a keynote speech by Billie Letts at a writers conference. Her novel *Where the Heart Is* had been chosen the week before by the Oprah Book Club, guaranteeing huge sales. The movie version of the novel would be released in a few weeks. So she was living the dream that we all hold in our hearts. Making the moment even more special, she spoke about the fact that a few years earlier, she sat in the audience at the same conference, a no-name conferee. Her very presence in the room made the dream seem that much more attainable, and the atmosphere was electrified. She could have recited bawdy limericks, and we'd have gone away inspired.

She didn't. Nor did she talk much about how it felt to be enjoying such a windfall of success. Instead, she told us about the process of writing the book and the struggle she went through when she was well into the book. She said she gave herself a daily goal of three pages. She couldn't begin her day until she met that goal. She couldn't even take a shower. Sometimes she went a few days without a shower. But she stayed in the chair, and she told us the book was made better by the effort.

Sue Grafton is another writer who stays in the chair. As you probably know, Grafton writes an enormously successful mystery series in which every title uses a letter of the alphabet. At this writing, she is up to *Q Is for Quarry*. She told me in an interview for a magazine article that she reaches a point where she thinks she won't make it to the end of the novel.

"I'm always convinced it's over," she said. "I worry that I'm out of juice, that I have nothing left to say." And yet she has managed to finish seventeen novels in the series, and I have faith she'll make it all the way to *Z Is for Zero*. (She's already chosen the title for the final one.)

These stories of perseverance rewarded give us hope that our dark moments are shared by even the most successful writers, of course, but more to the point, these stories show us that the struggle is part of the process.

Withholding Judgment

A common way to block yourself from completing a draft of a piece is to sit back and judge it before you have it on paper. It's a natural instinct. We make judgments every day. We're trained readers and writers, and we know what works. If a piece isn't working, we'll know.

Another way we block ourselves and limit the potential for our work is by judging how a piece should be realized. What it's about and where it should go. The first great wave of inspiration is exhilarating but it can be scary too. We want to grab control. We want to know the nature of this thing we're creating. And so we decide it's a story about our father, or we rush headlong through the plot and decide how it will end and what that will mean even as we're still scribbling the opening lines.

If you're still in the early stages of a first draft, it's not your job to make any conclusions about the piece. You don't yet know if it "sucks," because you don't yet know what it's about. The first strong wind of inspiration has passed. It may be time to break out the oars and row for a while. You also don't yet know what the piece is about—its themes, its range of dramatic possibilities. You will limit those possibilities by deciding too soon.

It's not our role at this time to say if something's good or bad, worth pursuing or destined for the wastebasket. We need to focus on the piece itself, listen to it, play with it, experiment with it. Keep putting words on paper. Keep adding ideas to the generative idea. Look for complications and possibilities. When you have a draft of something, or at least a good chunk of writing, you can allow yourself to assess its merits. For now, suspend your disbelief. Resist labeling it. Resist deciding too soon the direction the piece should take. Trust your imagination and the way your subconscious creates the piece.

The Grass Is Greener

As we've discussed, making your way through the middle of a project requires a certain amount of blind faith. It also requires withholding judgment. It also requires our focused attention. Another way we can get in our own way is by jumping from one project to the next at the first sign of difficulty. We begin to develop an idea into a draft of writing only to realize that several other ideas are much better. They're more interesting and exciting and we have a much firmer grasp of them. Well . . . maybe. Or we could be suffering from the-grass-is-greener syndrome.

When we're in the midst of writing a novel, the short story can have a powerful allure. The short story is so, well, short. It seems far less daunting than the novel we've undertaken. Or perhaps you're distracted from your novel by a memoir, with its simple demands of just telling what happened rather than having to make up everything. Of course, when we jump to the short story, we might feel constrained by the need for making every word count, for making every little action resonate within the whole of the story. When we jump to the memoir, we face research and flipping through old journals and trying to find ways to stick to the facts. Ah, so much easier to be able to create a fictional reality.

Sound familiar? We've all been there. As soon as we undertake project number two, project number one will look good again, or we'll think of a project number three. Some writers keep several projects going simultaneously until one rises to the fore. If you can balance projects in this way, feel free to do it. But if one rises to the fore, try to focus on that one. Simultaneous projects, as in romantic relationships, can be a way of avoiding a commitment.

Consider giving yourself a time limit for working on one project before moving to a new one. Also, be open to the possibility that project number two is asking to be folded into project number one. They might be related somehow in your subconscious. If the subjects and forms are radically different—such as an essay about life as a teacher and a short poem about your mother—finding the connection might not be easy, but be open to the possibility. Perhaps there's a thematic connection rather than a more obvious one directly involving the subject matter.

I wish I had a magic piece of advice to give you for how to keep moving on a project. We've looked at ways of getting started and developing a draft from a craft perspective, but often what stalls us has nothing to do with craft. More often it's a matter of our mental state. Completing a project requires persistence and tenacity. It also requires, at times, leaps of faith. Even if a piece seems aimless and pointless, trust that you're simply not at a place yet where the writing is ready to reveal its mysteries. And so we push on.

 ## Questions to Consider

1. As you work along in one project, is another one begging for your attention? Ask yourself if this other project is a means of avoiding a full commitment to the one at hand. Ask yourself, too, if the project causing the distraction might be part of the ongoing one or might provide some clue as to the true nature of the one in progress.

2. Do you tend to judge your writing projects too quickly? Do a quick count of the projects you've abandoned. Are any of them worth a fresh look?

3. If you're squirming to get out of your chair while writing, what's causing you to feel this way? Is it simply the desire to do something else, or are you facing a difficult scene or passage that at some level you're trying to avoid?

4. In what other parts of your life have you shown persistence and tenacity? Can you find a way to bring those qualities to your struggle with the ongoing piece?

Put It On Paper

PROMPT: Recall a time in your life when you judged something or some person without having all the facts. Write about it. What consequences arose from your premature judgment? How does recalling that experience make you feel now?

PROMPT: Here's a practice for suspending disbelief. Recall an outlandish situation you experienced or have heard about. Or, if none comes to mind, make one up. A really dumb thing that if someone told you it happened you wouldn't for a second believe them. Give yourself four or five pages to tell the story, doing your best to make it seem credible. Don't address the reader's possible doubts at any point. Act as if this is a believable story.

PROMPT: Your character got into trouble last night, and the car sits in the driveway with a fresh dent in it. He or she must explain to someone—parent, spouse, the car's owner—how the dent happened to find its way onto the car. Try to make the story seem both ridiculous and possible (if not probable). The listener's response is up to you: Incredulity? Confusion? Anger?

PROMPT: If you've got a piece underway but are beginning to feel it lag a bit, find a place in what you've written already that excites your interest. Perhaps it's a character or an image, a setting, even a subplot that appeals to you, even if the piece itself seems to have slowed down. Focus your energy there. You could expand its role in the story. Or you could freewrite about it. If you're smitten by a character, explore her background, even if you feel that what you write won't be included in the final piece. (Remember, we're avoiding those kinds of judgments at this point.) If you like an earlier scene, revisit it. Expand it, or perhaps jump ahead in your narrative to a place where the characters in that scene return. By focusing your energy and interest in this way, you can catch a renewed sense of engagement in the piece, and before you know it you're moving again.

PROMPT: Give yourself a time limit for getting through a rough spot in your piece of writing. You might say, I'll work on this section or this piece for the next five sessions. If it still seems blocked or flat, I'll let it go for a while. Make sure you give yourself enough time to get past the block—at least five sessions. If you have to put it away for a while, give yourself a time limit on when you'll revisit it.

PROMPT: If you're stuck, consider changing the time of day you usually use for writing. If you've been putting in an hour on your story before heading to work in the morning, write during your lunch break, or as soon as you get home in the evening. Also consider changing where you write. If at a computer, take a notepad to a park or a library. New times and locations and routines for writing can spark new interest.

PROMPT: Consider how you start and end your writing sessions. Do you write until you're exhausted? If so, consider stopping while you're still feeling energetic about the project. Ernest Hemingway made famous his method of stopping each session in the middle of a sentence, so he'd know just how to start the new session. This approach might work for you.

PROMPT: Write about an act of faith you've committed in your life—faith that you'd land a job, find a satisfying relationship, even something as simple as your team winning a Little League game. Explore the experience and your feelings at the time. Why did you believe as you did and what forces sustained that belief? How did the act of believing influence the outcome?

PROMPT: Create a fictional situation in which a character commits an act of faith, believing in something despite evidence to the contrary or no evidence at all. If you want, stack the deck against the character, providing plenty of evidence that he or she appears to be acting foolishly and ignoring "facts" that undermine the belief. Give the piece a happy ending.

PROMPT: Spend at least three sessions practicing the "stay in the chair" method. Set a timer for your session, and write whatever you want, perhaps responding to a prompt in this book. Do not *for any reason* get up from the chair. Turn off the phone, shut down your e-mail, tell family members that for the next half hour or whatever time you choose you are not to be disturbed unless someone is facing a life-or-death situation. If the idea you're exploring stalls before you finish, begin a new one or simply write about writing or describe the room in which you're working. Your goal is to practice staying in the chair.

Part II
Evaluating Ideas

Chapter Six

Stoking the Fire

A s we move deeper into the project we're developing, we sometimes sense it going flat. It lacks the inspiration that kept us going through the early stages of creation, and even though we're willing to suspend judgment, as we discussed in the previous chapter, we can't shake the notion that the piece needs more of something. Sometimes we don't make this discovery until we've finished a complete draft, even a complete piece. Our great idea that sent us racing to a notepad in the middle of the night, the one that scorched our fevered brains through exhilarating sessions at the computer, now lays on the page, a ghost of what we hoped it would be.

For an idea to work well, it needs to grow, to complicate itself with more ideas. By complication, I mean a second idea that extends or enlarges the first. A very basic example:

Idea: Boy meets girl. They fall in love.

Complication: Their families have a long-standing feud and hate each other. Their parents would forbid a marriage. And so the lovers get married in secret.

Complication: The boy gets into a fight with the girl's cousin, who is killed. The boy must run away.

Complication: The girl's father, unaware she has married the boy, orders her to marry the son of a well-placed family.

You get the idea.

Shakespeare could have pushed the single conflict between the families to its natural conclusion, but he complicates the story of star-crossed love by bringing in larger questions about human nature and society. Meanwhile, he pushes his lovers further and further away from each other.

It's tough to know all of these complications when we first sit down to explore an idea. We discover them as we write. That's why it's important to work on a promising idea long enough to explore its possibilities. We must give ourselves to make discoveries, to add new ideas to the generative idea.

Here's another example. We're working on a story about a woman whose boss is making her life miserable. His demands are impossible to meet. We create several scenes showing the boss unfairly and caustically criticizing the protagonist. Then we write a few more. And a few more. She works harder, but the fatigue caused by the pressure and the shaky judgment caused by her lessening confidence make her prone to error. She talks to a colleague, then to a friend or two. The story progresses in this way, but the conflict is, for the most part, flat-lining.

I see this type of story time and again when I read for conferences and contests. A strong idea that is full of drama and conflict becomes a one-note wonder, in which the writer presents the same conflict between the same characters in largely the same way and with the same tone until the story has lost its punch. The initial conflict is played to its inevitable conclusion. It's the kind of story that makes inexperienced readers fumble for what to say. They often question the pace, saying, "It seems slow in the second half." And, indeed, it does. But the problem isn't the pace. The problem is a lack of invention. The initial idea isn't developed with more ideas. There are no surprises, no complications.

Adding Ideas

If you're feeling your piece go stale, or if readers aren't responding to it in the way you hoped, step back and evaluate how you've developed and complicated the initial idea. How many scenes or how many pages are spent making the same point or eliciting the same response from the reader? Grab some colored markers and underline in a single color all the sentences dedicated to one conflict. If the conflict shifts or if it's complicated by new information, grab a different marker and keep underlining. When you've finished, step back and see the result in living color. Perhaps the problem with your "dull idea" or "bad idea" is simply that it hasn't taken the next step into something larger or deeper. The problem at the end exists in the same place as when we started. Boss= bad. Protagonist=good. Conflict: stay or go.

Another way to hone your skills at spotting a one-note story is to read a favorite story several times (and by "story" I mean essay or article or screenplay or whatever form you're working in). We'll get into this strategy at greater depth in the next section, but it warrants mention here. Mark the turns in the story, the deepening of character or theme, the shifts in conflict, the complications, the surprises, the passages that build suspense. Use the same color scheme you used in marking your own story. How well do they match? Does the story you've read have a greater variety of colors than the one you wrote?

If you conclude you've got a one-note wonder on your hands, it's time to add ideas. Getting ideas at this stage is much the same as getting the generative idea for the piece. You imagine possibilities. You ask "what if?" What if our hapless employee has quit her last two jobs, having disliked or failed at them for various reasons? Staying at this job and satisfying the tyrant takes on greater importance. The stakes have been raised. Or what if she's raising children on her own, or her husband is in law school and she's the only breadwinner? Her pressures at work spill into her relationships at home, expanding the range of the story. Or what if you gradually show that the boss's complaints are justified, reversing the reader's expectations? Or what if she discovers the boss's marriage is failing or that he's working through some personal grief? Now there's a matter of humanity involved, a question of how much sympathy she'll allow to excuse his behavior. Or what if you changed the relationship between the characters? What if the tyrannical boss is her father? Now we have a new element, a father-daughter theme that complicates the initial idea of a workplace story.

You see my point. Imagine new possibilities. Push the story to its next logical step. Deepen the characters. Imagine the situation from a new perspective. Raise the stakes. And raise them again. How can the situation be more distressing for your protagonist? How can the outcome be of greater consequence? How can she, in attempting to extricate herself, plunge herself even deeper into confusion or misery?

Here's another example: We have an idea for an article about a grand old building scheduled for the wrecking ball in our hometown. We research the building's history and talk to the people involved in the demolition. We find nothing especially surprising, and there seems to be no conflict about whether or not to tear it down. We rhapsodize about the building's former glory, even as we admit the need for the old to make way for the new. In the end, we end up with a nicely written yet utterly predictable elegy that never rises above our initial conception of the piece. It's a one-note wonder.

A complication would have helped. We needed another element, perhaps a new building going up elsewhere in town that could supply a comparison. Instead of interviewing only the city planners, we could have rounded up stories from elderly people who remember the building's glory days. Perhaps these stories could be contrasted by reactions of local teens who think the old place was pretty much a dump. Perhaps we could have written an extended piece of satire, in the tradition of Swift's classic "A Modest Proposal." We could have called the piece "Good Riddance."

Again, the point is clear. By sticking too close to the original idea rather than adding new ideas, we ended up with a predictable bit of one-note nostalgia. As with the story about the woman's conflict at work, we needed to ask "what if?" Raise the stakes. Consider new approaches, perspectives, and tones. Place the idea within the context of something larger.

Another way of finding these ideas is to search your feelings about the piece. Ask yourself: Is my idea fresh? Have I read pieces like this before? How is mine unique? Does the piece reflect my true feelings about the building? What *are* my feelings about the building? Am I truly sad, or am

I conjuring a somber tone simply because I feel it's expected? (Remember the lesson from chapter two about writing more sentences than are required.) How can I more accurately reflect my true feelings about the subject? What ideas could be added to this idea to bring it more to life, to make it fresher, more engaging so that readers will enjoy the experience rather than be run through the standard grid of emotions and ideas?

Sometimes we must be willing to go way beyond the initial conception. The generative idea took us to a certain place, and now we must move from there. For example, in our story of the woman and her boss, we may need to ask, "What if she quits?" Where does the story go from here? Though our initial idea focused on the situation at work, leading up to an anti-climactic showdown at the end, the situation with the boss could be condensed into a few opening paragraphs, sending us boldly on our way into a completely different story, one involving the search for a new job or one focusing on the character's need for a more significant life change. We'll spend more time on this strategy in chapter eight. But as we think about adding ideas, keep your mind open to shifting the story in a new direction. When you read interviews with writers about how a book evolved, often you'll learn that the generative idea is a tiny part of the completed project. That idea was simply an avenue toward others. And the writer was willing to explore those others, to consciously pursue them.

Why Just the One Note?

Sometimes our stories are limited because we really don't want to broaden their range, but for various reasons we can't admit this fact to ourselves. One reason we don't want to consider other possibilities is our rush to publish. We finish a draft of a story, massage it a bit, give it a quick edit, a polish and a proofread, and it's out the door, sailing to the doors of magazine editors. We haven't lived in the world of the story long enough. We haven't imagined its possibilities, taken risks with it. The most common complaint I hear from friends who edit magazines is that they see "too many early drafts." They reject these stories, leaving the writers to wonder where they went wrong.

The antidote to this illness is simple: Don't be so quick to declare a story finished. We all enjoy getting published, but make sure you're sending out fully realized work. Give yourself time to live in the world of the story, to carry your characters around in your head. If you're writing an essay or memoir, give yourself time to know for sure you've said what you want to say, that your piece is developed to its potential.

Some writers send stories off too quickly because they suffer from commitment phobia. When the generative idea has been pushed to its natural conclusion, the story is finished. They have no desire to break it apart or start over after page three, thank you very much. These drastic measures require more commitment than they're willing to make. They either file away the story as a bad idea or do a quick, nip-and-tuck edit to superficially address the reader's concerns. The question then becomes: How important is it to these writers to tell this story? Is the problem a lack of invention or a lack of commitment, a passionate need to put these words on paper? These are questions we must ask ourselves.

We also might block a story's emotional and thematic range because broadening that range requires us to venture into psychologically troubled waters. Here's an anecdote to illustrate. A few years ago, at a writers retreat where I teach every year, my group read and discussed a student's short story about a woman whose distant, critical mother carps at her constantly throughout a weekend visit. The protagonist rolls her eyes at these complaints, occasionally shooting a wry rejoinder at her mother before, in the end, the mother leaves, and the daughter sighs with relief, a bit sad that the relationship isn't more loving. The story was well written, full of sharply observed details. The group praised its strengths, as groups tend to do. It was clear to me, however, that the story was not fully realized, that after all the rejoinders and interesting details it didn't amount to much. The story wanted to be more than it was.

I asked the writer about her intentions for the piece and about the relationship between the mother and daughter. The writer said she simply wanted to present the relationship and to show the daughter putting up with the mother's constant criticism, which she had lived with all her life but which now lacked much meaning for her. It was the story of a daughter's triumph, of her reaching a new level of maturity.

"Why don't the criticisms bother the daughter anymore?" I asked.

"Because she's older now," the writer answered. "She's outgrown the need for her mother's approval." (This writer, a smart, dour woman in her early sixties, didn't much care for me, and, like the daughter in the story, rolled her eyes at any critical comments, however kindly phrased, I made in the workshop.)

"I'm just not sure if that's enough to move the story forward," I said. "She doesn't care at the beginning, and she doesn't care at the end. What do you want the reader to take from that?"

"I'm just showing a relationship," the writer snapped.

I said, "What if the daughter did care? How would the story be different if the mother's criticism hurt the daughter deeply? What if the daughter is just pretending not to care and secretly would love to have her mother's approval?"

The writer burst into tears.

When she regained her composure, she told us that the story was based on her relationship with her own mother, who is very critical, and though the writer doesn't show how much those criticisms have hurt her through the years, she has the emotional scars to prove it.

I wish I could tell you that I knew all of this, and with the cunning grace of Socrates I guided her through my questions to discover the true nature of her story. But I would be lying. I was just fishing around, trying to open the writer to various possibilities, trying to find out what made the story worth telling for her, looking for the chaos beneath the polished exterior of the story. That's what we do when a story needs more, an extra *something*, but we're not sure what it is. We fish around. We ask ourselves questions. We experiment. The workshop student had decided from the start that the story was about a daughter putting up with, while no longer caring about, her mother's hectoring comments. She closed the door on the possibility that she really needed to write about how much a daughter did care, how much she resented her mother's life-long emotional stinginess.

Again, sometimes our first idea is simply a way to get at a better one. Sometimes it's simply a single facet of a larger jewel of writing. When we don't explore and discover the other facets, our story doesn't end up as a diamond. It ends up as a flat rock.

If your story feels flat, ask yourself if there's an aspect of it you're hesitant to explore. Is the one note simply the first note of a song you're afraid to sing? If so, you have a decision to make. I'm not beseeching you to sing that song. That's your choice. But you've found the reason why a story with a good strong idea isn't lifting to great literary heights.

I'd like to end this section by telling you that after the beautiful moment in the workshop, the writer and I became good friends. We had a good-bye hug, she returned home and revised the story, which she then sent to me. It was great. But that would be too obvious and familiar a note to strike. (It also wouldn't be true.) I don't know if she revised the piece or if she went home from the retreat and confronted her mother. I'll leave that next step in the tale to you. What do you think might happen?

Questions to Consider

1. Have you added new ideas to your first one? Have you complicated your initial premise in an interesting way? If not, are you sensing the need for more?
2. If you're feeling that your work in progress needs new ideas, what's holding you back?
3. Are you limiting the scope of your piece on purpose—either to avoid the challenge of a more complicated piece or because you need to feel in control of it? What might happen if you relinquished control for a while?
4. Are the pieces you've declared finished really as good as you can make them? Of course, we need to let go of a piece sometimes, to move on, but review the work you've sent out in hopes of getting published. Is it your best work? Have you given yourself enough time with it?

Put It On Paper

PROMPT: Brainstorm a list of complications for your work in progress. Make it a big list—at least fifteen items. Go crazy with it. At least three of the complications must be preposterous, requiring of you (and your reader) huge leaps of faith.

PROMPT: Describe your story in two sentences. Now add a third sentence, introducing a new element, even one that may not seem appropriate. For example, the workshop student could write: "This story focuses on a weekend visit by a woman's mother, who has always been very critical. During the weekend, the daughter realizes she's outgrown the need for her mother's approval." As a third element, she might add, "As the mother loads up her car to leave, the daughter insists that they go shopping together." Try this prompt several times, playing with possibilities for the third element.

PROMPT: Create a new element of the story that is being kept secret by one of the characters. Allude to this secret somewhere in the first scene. As you move ahead, slowly reveal the secret, one that adds another complication to the story. You needn't know the secret yourself when you start writing. Allow yourself to discover it as you write.

PROMPT: Take a day off from the work in progress and brainstorm ideas for a new project. Again, make it a long list. Put the list away and return to the work in progress at your next writing session. At some point, pull out the list of ideas for a new project. Choose one item from the list and find a way to weave it into the work in progress.

PROMPT: If you feel your scenes are too similar in their objective, add a random element. The more random the better. Brainstorm a list of possibilities. Or, if you feel you won't be random enough, consider these possibilities: a fortune cookie, a necklace, pruning shears, a flat tire, a grocery receipt, a ferret, a negligee, a park bench, a glass of water, M&Ms.

PROMPT: Outline your piece as you see it now. No need for long annotations in your outline. Just use a word or phrase to describe each part or scene. Then, outline a piece with the same subject or premise but change the approach—its structure, its events, its outcomes, its point of view, etc. Outline it again, this time with yet another approach. And again. Allow the piece to be illogical, even outrageous. When you're finished, review your outlines, looking for elements that can be added to the original outline.

PROMPT: Play "Raise the Stakes." Add a new element to your piece that makes the premise or situation more significant in some way. More dire for the protagonist. More meaningful. More life-changing in its outcome. If you're working on a personal essay or memoir, look for greater consequences in the situation. Is the experience you're exploring a pivotal one in your life? Does it resonate beyond your life in ways that may touch the reader's own life?

PROMPT: After you've raised the stakes in the previous prompts, look ahead in your piece for a place to raise them again.

PROMPT: Rewrite a scene from the work in progress to change the tone in a significant way. If the scene is fraught with anger, for example, present that anger in a humorous tone. Experiment with ways to make the scene funny. Or, if your scene involves a shocking revelation, emphasize the beauty of the moment.

PROMPT: Make a surprising move. If your character reacts in a predictable way to an event, change the reaction. A man driving home from a wonderful first date doesn't whistle a love song or dance in the street. He stops at a grocery store, carefully selecting his items. Or, in an essay, rather than summarize your response to an event you've just finished dramatizing, shift to a new subject, bringing in some fresh element.

PROMPT: Describe a process. This exercise is a standard in technical-writing courses. Students explain the steps involved in doing something, such as fixing a flat tire or installing a water heater. Spend part of a writing session describing a process. Then look for ways of weaving this process into the work in progress. For example in her essay on how to write the lyric essay, Brenda Miller describes how to make challah bread. She uses the process to enlarge the essay and make her points about craft in a more lyric way. In fiction, describing a process can have the same effect, the most famous being the chapters in *Moby Dick* that describe the techniques of whaling. Your fictional character, rather than react to his wife's leaving in the typical ways, might carefully wax his car. Don't look for obvious parallels when deciding on which process to describe. Choose one you know well or one you can research.

PROMPT: Spend a page or two with a minor character or, in nonfiction, a minor person. Expound a bit upon her or him. Give us background details and a detailed physical description. Look for ways to expand the role of this person in your piece.

PROMPT: Choose your favorite part of the piece—a line of dialogue or detail or a sentence that strikes you as especially good. Freewrite about this part, letting yourself take off in a new direction. You may decide after you finish that the part needs to remain exactly as it is, or you may discover a new mine of inspiration.

PROMPT: Change a relationship in the piece. If your character is having a problem with a neighbor, for example, make that neighbor a high school sweetheart of your character's wife. If you're writing a personal essay, explore a new attitude about one of the people in the piece. If you've showered your sister with loving praise throughout the essay, for example, admit that her habit of deciding where everyone must sit at Thanksgiving dinner bothers you. Explore that feeling a bit. Or, if your essay involves plenty of snipes at an ex-spouse, spend a few paragraphs mentioning the spouse's endearing qualities. (Surely there's at least one!)

PROMPT: Give your character some surprising news that shifts the natural course of the story. It could be good news or bad news, but it must be news that requires a new plan of action for the character. If you're writing nonfiction, add some type of news to the mix, even if it seems unrelated at the moment. Your task will be to expand or deepen the piece enough to accommodate such news.

Chapter Seven

Exploding the Idea

Pablo Picasso said, "Every act of creation is first an act of destruction." I wasn't there when he said it, and I have no idea what he meant. He may have been in a bad mood. But I've always thought the statement sounded pretty cool. It makes the creative artist seem powerful and iconoclastic, smashing with the hammer of artistic vision the statues of conformity. As writers, we do have that power, if we're willing to use it.

For our purposes, however, we're going to use the quote to begin a discussion of destroying our initial idea. As we've discussed in previous chapters, sometimes the generative idea for a piece is more an avenue to richer ideas than an end in itself. At those times, we must be willing to let go of our initial premise. We have to explode the idea. In some ways, to echo Picasso, this is the first act of creation.

There are few comments more deflating than when your readers agree that your 25-page story "really begins on page 24." We've worked hard on those first 23 pages. They're honed and crafted and have a lot of good lines in them. And now we're supposed to believe they're only so much throat-clearing? A mere prelude to the *real* story? Sometimes, the answer is yes.

At such times, we must remember that we wouldn't have achieved the real start of the story if we hadn't written what came before. Our initial premise led us to literary gold, even though now it must be discarded. I had this experience with a story I wrote a few years ago. It concerns a mother and daughter who are lost in L.A., far from their Ohio home. I worked hours on extended dialogues between the characters, took great pains to deliver the exposition in an unobtrusive way. I had conceived the story much like a play, focusing on subtle shifts of character as the mother and daughter conversed. Near the end, two rough-looking guys enter the doughnut shop where the story takes place. My plan was to have a brief encounter with the men and for the foursome to leave together at the end. Several readers said they felt the story spark to life when the two guys enter. But that was at the end! This was a Beckett-like story of tightly woven dialogue, not some tale of women being picked up by truckers. Hel-loo. Tightly woven Beckett-like dialogue here. You folks are missing the point.

I let the story sit for some months. Then I read it with a fresh view. Then I reread the readers' comments. They were right. My pages of tightly woven, Beckett-like dialogue were cut extensively. I now could see that much of it was self-conscious and tiresome anyway. The tension between the mother and daughter as they sat in a doughnut shop wasn't enough to carry the story. After five pages or so, the story felt static. In the revised version, the men enter the doughnut shop on the top of page two. The foursome is out the door by page seven. But those weeks of working the dialogue helped me know the mother and daughter, and my knowledge of them led to surprising turns in the revised story, turns I don't know I'd have imagined if I hadn't had such a rounded understanding of the characters.

When you find yourself in a similar place, listen to what your readers tell you. If only one reader advises to start with the ending, give the piece to a second reader or put it away for a while. Your first reader may be imposing his or her own vision of your story world and is stating the way he or she would handle the material. If a second reader offers similar advice, it's worth considering. If the second reader says something more like "It seemed kind of slow to me," ask for specific places where it seemed most interesting. If the reader points to the place the first reader suggested to begin the story, you have a decision to make.

Lopping away a big chunk of story isn't easy, and requires consideration. Put the story away and move on to a new one for a while. Give the story at least a month to cool off, preferably longer. In fact, set a date for rereading the story. Write it on your calendar. The date will ensure you don't read the story sooner than is helpful, and it also reminds you the story is there. We sometimes forget about our stories for so long that we have a great deal of trouble bringing them back to life. And so the deadline works in two ways, making sure you don't return too soon or wait too long.

When you return to the story, note in the margins where it's working and where it needs help. Are the readers correct in their assessment of the sections that could be cut or be significantly condensed? Read the story again, beginning at the place where it might be made to start. Does it make a strong opening? What needs to be pulled from the cut material and how much can be set free?

Letting Go

It takes a certain amount of courage to cut away pages of a story. Don't forget to put these pages in your idea file. They may contain the seed of another story idea or lines of dialogue or arresting images that you don't want to throw away. But when you've cut the pages, they're gone. Don't agonize over them or rationalize ways of returning them to the story.

Another reason it's tough to explode your idea and let go of it is that the pages, once written, once developed and honed, take on an inevitability. They *seem* right. They feel organic to the piece, simply because they've been there for so long. We've read and reread them. We expect them to appear, and we recognize their rhythms. In fact, in some ways we don't even see them anymore. We take their presence for granted.

Putting a story away for a while can lessen that sense of inevitability. When we can read with a fresh vision, the story loses its familiarity. At that time, ask yourself if this or that section is necessary, if this or that event signals a new and better course for the story. Are there places where you must, to paraphrase Faulkner, kill your darlings? Just as certain scenes or sentences take on an inevitability and thus stay past their welcome, scenes and sentences can stay too long because they are favorites. Usually we like them because they possess a brio that reflects well on us as writers. They make us sound good. But are they relics of an earlier vision for the story? Are they there *only* because they make you sound good? If so, they must be killed.

Letting a piece go where it wants to go also can be difficult for us. Our initial premise dictates a certain structure, a clear narrative path. And yet, when a piece is well underway, it takes on a will of its own. I'm not one of those writers who talk a lot about characters taking over or telling the writer what to write. I've always found such talk a bit fallacious and self-aggrandizing, turning the creative process (and therefore, the creative artist) into an inspired genius in touch with mysterious forces beyond the powers of normal folk.

At the same time, I don't agree with Nabokov's famous comment about characters being his "galley slaves" either. The creative process isn't just a mechanized act of will, an application of learned techniques. Our subconscious minds, the myth-making power of our imaginations, do come into play. Conscious craft and subconscious artistry unite in a piece, granting it a power we can't always control. I don't know that it's a matter of characters taking over. I think it's that at some point the story moves along its own path. It knows what it wants to be, even when we have different ideas about what it *should* be.

Creative writing is such an intuitive act that it's tough to make this point in a concrete way. To recognize when you're forcing a story away from its natural course, look for places where it begins to sound awkward to your artistic ear. Do you find yourself at some level asking if the character would really do that? Does a scene end with one character having the last word in a way that seems false? Does the analysis of a key event in your personal essay serve more to make you look innocent than to provide an authentic insight? Trust your instincts. Perhaps you're working against your own piece. You've moved beyond your initial premise into territory you may not want to visit, but your uneasiness is suggesting you have to explode that generative idea and move on. Responding to that uneasiness, even consciously feeling it, requires spending enough time on a piece to really hear what it's telling you.

At first, we may feel uneasy about an aspect of the piece in a faint way. We may feel it sometimes and not at others as we read. Sometimes it takes another reader to point it out, causing us to say, "I sort of wondered about that part. It never seemed quite right to me."

For example, we're trying to end a scene but nothing works, nothing feels like the natural place to stop. Whatever final lines we write don't have the ring of finality. If you want to say that the characters have taken over, that they've decided they don't want to stop talking, fine. I would phrase it more along the lines of the story's asserting its own course. The falseness enters because we are sticking too closely to our idea of where the story must go. We say to ourselves, "This isn't an important scene. It's just a transitional scene, taking me from this event to that event. I can't spend ten pages on a transitional scene." And yet, something about that transitional scene remains unresolved. If we trust our intuition, we allow the scene to find its own resolution. Perhaps a better idea is appearing before your eyes. But often, we cut the scene short. We stick to our original conception of the piece. And yet, something about the ending of that scene bothers us every time we read it. Something doesn't seem right about it.

Other Clues

Is one of the characters drawing your interest in unexpected ways? If you find yourself drawn to a character's voice or to the character's actions and behavior, consider the possibility that the story is really about that character, rather than the one you deemed the protagonist in your original conception of the piece. You may need to shift your focus. How would your piece change if you moved that character to the foreground? Does the character provide a complication, as we discussed in the previous chapter, or does the character warrant a major change in the design of the story?

Of course, minor characters sometimes possess a certain charm within a limited role and draw attention to themselves, even drawing the reader's interest away from the main characters. In her wonderful book *Get That Novel Written!*, Donna Levin calls this "the Barney Fife Syndrome," after the bumbling deputy on the old *The Andy Griffith Show*. If the show were recast to feature Barney, however, it would have become a slapstick farce rather than a homey, feel-good comedy. Small doses of Barney worked better, giving the show a comedic range without making it a completely different type of show.

To extend Donna's point by returning to television (not that any of us ever watches television), the show *Happy Days* began as a quirky and somewhat textured evocation of the 1950s. It had a quiet charm and an ideal protagonist to render that charm: Richie Cunningham. A minor character named Fonzie added a nice note of rebellion, a counterpoint to good-guy Richie. Fonzie was '50s-cool, and yet his obvious personal limitations added an element of melancholy. The audience sensed this was the hey-day for such guys, and life would never be so good for them again. The audience loved the Fonz, and so the writers shifted the focus to emphasize him. But he was a stereotype, really, not a character who offered a lot of range. The new approach constricted all the other characters, turning them into broad stereotypes too. The show lost its quiet charm and became a caricature of itself.

The point is that shifting your focus will have consequences for your story. Try to determine if this character requires you to explode the original idea, or if you've simply happened upon an engaging character who adds a new layer of charm to the story. Keeping the character in a limited role can be difficult, especially when readers laud the character. "I love the woman who smokes on the train!" they'll say with delight. What writer can resist such delight from readers?

If a minor character is drawing the most attention but you're sure it's not his or her story, examine your protagonist. Is he or she compelling enough? Perhaps the minor character is simply spilling into the story's missing center. It may be time, as we discussed in the previous chapter, to raise the stakes for the protagonist.

It need not be a character drawing attention. It could be a theme, a subplot, a place. Your drama set in the Rockies is dwarfed, literally, by the setting. Perhaps the setting needs to be pushed to the foreground, made a character in its own right. Perhaps the story has less to do with the conflict between your characters than a conflict between the characters and the place they live.

The same situation can occur in essays and memoirs. You want to focus on a particular person, and yet another person keeps wedging into the spotlight. And readers seem to respond to this person. They're curious about him or her. You find yourself responding too. Perhaps your essay is a recollection of a particular place where you played as a child—a grove of trees or the sprawling backyard of a long-forgotten friend. It's also a meditation on childhood, and on the power of imagination that dims with time. You have children of your own now and conceive of your essay as a comparison between where they play and where you played, using the place as a metaphor for childhood itself.

Except that the long-forgotten friend keeps butting in. You find yourself describing the friend for pages, recalling specific summer days and the games the two of you played. You remember in sudden, sharp detail the look on the friend's face when it was time for you to go home to eat dinner. You find yourself struggling to get back to your idea about the play areas and watching your own kids. Every time you end a passage about the friend, you sense a need for more. Perhaps it's time to put aside the essay about childhood places of play and focus on an essay about a long-forgotten friendship.

Try not to see the need to explode your idea, blowing it up and beginning a new course, as a failure. It's not. It's another way of perceiving— and building upon—the possibilities of the original idea. The explosion creates all sorts of wonderful fragments that can be new ideas in themselves. In his book *Revision, A Creative Approach to Writing and Rewriting Fiction*, David Michael Kaplan writes of re-vision, seeing a project in a new way. We often think of revision as simply adding some details here and there, polishing the language, making sure the backstory is presented gracefully, maybe even cutting some of it that no longer seems necessary. But this tinkering is not really revision. Remember the old saying that "It's not revision until you're cutting something that hurts." You may be cutting only a favorite phrase or line of dialogue, or you may be cutting the first half of the piece, because that half is part of an idea that was simply a stepping stone to a better idea.

Questions to Consider

1. Are you feeling blocked on your work in progress? Are you blocking yourself by refusing to move beyond your original idea for the piece?
2. Where does the piece seem to be working best? Where is it most genuine? Do these sections grow out of the original idea or do they hint of better ideas, ones that move beyond the original idea?
3. Is one aspect of the piece trying to dominate it? Is it possible that the original idea needs to be discarded or perhaps refocused to allow this aspect to surface or develop in the foreground?
4. Is it time to look at your original idea with new eyes?

Put It On Paper

PROMPT: Review your work in progress, looking for places that concern you, ones that don't seem to be working. Rather than cutting them, explore them by writing another page or two. You could extend them, writing beyond what you have done so far. You could write *about* them, explaining why you find them troublesome. Don't put pressure on the pages you write. Use them as a way of spending more time on a place in your piece that needs more attention.

PROMPT: Review you work in progress, looking for places that particularly interest you. Explore them by writing another page or two. As with the previous prompt, you could extend them or simply write about why you like them.

PROMPT: Imagine that you've lost—due to a computer failure or a literary burglar—the entire work in progress. If necessary, hide anything you've written on the piece from yourself. Begin again. Write a few pages. Some of it you'll be able to write from memory, while some of it you'll have to create afresh. When you finish, compare the new version to the "lost" one. How do they differ? What discoveries did you make in the new version?

PROMPT: Go through work you've done in the past, whether or not it's finished, that you feel didn't quite work in the way you hoped. Choose one piece and reread it. Can you find places where the story goes awry? Are there places where you made a wrong turn? Focusing on those places, write new material, allowing the piece to push off in a fresh direction.

PROMPT: Pick another piece from your pile. Try to read it without thinking about the goals for the piece, your intentions when you wrote it. Read it, if possible, as if someone else wrote it. Then write an analysis of the piece, its strengths and weaknesses. Sometimes we find that a story we thought was about one idea was truly about a different idea.

PROMPT: Let's go back to television for a moment. (And you thought this was a high-minded literary book.) You have been called in to create a spin-off of your work in progress or from a completed piece. Your new show focuses on a single character or setting or event from the ongoing work. Choose the focus of your spin-off and write a few pages. Do you find it more or less engaging than the longer work?

PROMPT: Spend a session on an alternative scene or version of the piece in progress. For example, if your piece leads to a climactic scene in which the protagonist reaches a new level of insight, deny her that insight. Have her reach a completely different conclusion. For example, in the classic story "Araby" by James Joyce, the protagonist goes to a carnival to buy something for a girl with whom he is smitten. The story leads to the moment when the boy reaches a booth where he hopes to find the right gift. While standing there he realizes he has been foolishly romantic in his quest and walks away empty-handed. As an alternative, the author might have allowed the boy to select a gift and bring it home without having reached any conclusions about his emotional state.

PROMPT: You've been told to condense the piece to two pages. Everything must go but the best, most essential, parts of the piece. Choose what remains. The two pages need not be self-contained or even make sense when read from start to finish. You might choose six lines of dialogue from one scene, a one-sentence description from another page, and so on. When you have made your selections, write a short explanation to explain them. As you're doing this exercise, be mindful of what you value most in the piece and look for ways of building on those elements so that the entire piece reaches that level of interest for you.

PROMPT: Loosen the reins on a character by writing a scene (or recalling a time, if you're writing nonfiction) in which the character acts in a way that contradicts what you've presented already. Your father-figure, for example, who has shown patience with a difficult situation could be seen whipping a fickle toaster against a wall. The point of this exercise is not necessarily to show many sides of a character. Our goal is to relax our own assumptions and expectations about a character, to let them act on their own for a while.

PROMPT: Spend a session exploring your piece with a different thematic goal in mind. For example, if your story seems to be about people struggling with the tenets of their conservative religious training, push these folks and their situation forward with a new focus, perhaps their struggle with the morays of the small, southern town where they live.

Chapter Eight

Reading Is
Fundamental

The author W.P. Kinsella (*Shoeless Joe, Box Socials*) tells his students that they have to write forty stories before they can write one about the death of a family member. His reason: He reads too many dead grandparent stories. Allow me to augment his dictum a bit. Don't try to write a short story until you've read fifty of them, preferably a hundred. Don't try to write a novel until you've read fifty of them, preferably a hundred. The same is true for scripts, essays, poems, and so on.

I'm only being partly serious in my statement. If you feel compelled to write, I won't truly recommend delaying the urge. But when you begin that short story, begin your process of reading fifty stories. I cannot stress enough that reading is fundamental to learning how to write. In fact, if there's a *secret* to learning to write well—other than, of course, writing and writing and writing—it's reading, reading, reading. Nearly all of the good writers I've ever known love to read. Many writers who continued to struggle along in trying to master the craft did not read a lot. A personal observation. Agree or don't. That's been my experience.

Why Read

Reading adds richness to your language and to your imagination. By reading good work, we learn the sound of good writing. We learn how to handle the elements of craft. We cultivate an aesthetic, developing and honing our opinions about what works and why it works. We learn about—and thereby more truly inherit—the tradition in which we're working. We even can steal techniques, ideas, and phrases from the masters.

I've noticed that apprentices who don't progress as writers haven't read much. The language of their work lacks richness. They have not cultivated a critical aesthetic that would make them good editors of their own work. They make the same mistakes time and again. They don't know the sound of good writing.

Yes, there are those blessed with exceptionally rich material—life experience that supplies their work with a power that makes for compelling stories all by itself. Or they have a natural sense of voice that connects with readers in an almost primal way. You probably know some writers of this type. They haven't read much, but their work transcends their limitations of craft. Most of us, however, must work to unearth our material and to discover our voices. Part of that work, of learning the craft, involves reading.

Reading feeds your imagination. It puts you in touch with the language part of your brain. It develops your vocabulary. It teaches you the names of things. It shows you how successful writers work, the techniques they use to develop characters and structure stories. It places you within the ongoing literary discussion of the times in which you live. In fact, I feel safe in saying that if you don't read widely and well, you won't be as good a writer as you can be. Amass, if you will, evidence to the contrary, and I'll still believe that reading is a fundamental element of writing.

Through the years I've heard a number of apprentice writers claim they're as good as this or that much more accomplished writer. They'll decry the "crap that's being published today" while their own work is ignored. It's not tough, I'll admit, to find plenty of examples of published work that was better left unpublished, but usually when I hear these writers make such claims I'm much more painfully aware of what these writers are missing, the undetected differences between what they're doing and what the more successful writer is doing. They lack the critical faculties to notice those differences, and the lack of those critical faculties makes improvement a very slow process.

If you believe that most of what you read is crap (and you're reading well published books and magazines), perhaps you simply don't like to read, which could mean you really don't like to write all that much. You're pursuing a craft for which you have no genuine passion. You may be writing, therefore, for the wrong reasons. I hear writers, for example, say that they don't read literary magazines because "they're so boring," and yet those writers are trying to publish in those magazines.

If you want to be a good writer, you have to read a lot and you have to learn to read like a writer. It's that simple. If you want to be able to assess and develop your writing ideas more effectively, you have to read widely and well. By reading, you develop your critical aesthetic. You learn what works and what doesn't. You learn what's been done and what's been done to death. You learn the techniques that work and those that don't. You learn the techniques that may have worked in the past but no longer work.

In short: If you want to be a good judge of your ideas and understand why they're working or why they're not working, you have to read.

What You Read

If you're going to learn how good writing sounds and how it works, and if you're going to learn how to assess your ideas, you'll have to read good writing. Inferior work is not going to teach you a lot. Read the great stylists and the great storytellers. Read classic as well as contemporary writers. Read writers who work in various forms. If you write fiction, don't limit yourself to reading only fiction.

Do read, however, the masters of the form in which you write. If you are working on a mystery novel, you should know the masters of the genre. Without a clear sense of the tradition in which you're working, it's tough to write well. You'll spend a great deal of time making discoveries that have been made many times before you. Sometimes, of course, we have to discover something for ourselves to understand it fully, but learning the basic lessons of the craft can involve much more time in trial and error if you don't bother to read what's been done before.

Some apprentices worry that they'll be tempted to imitate the masters if they spend time reading them. The old "anxiety of influence." They fear they won't find their own unique voice. They fear their ideas will lack originality. This concern, I think, is vastly overrated. Most apprentices can benefit much more from that type of influence than by trying to avoid it. Your own voice will emerge. Your own ideas will break away from the master's ideas. In the meantime, you'll be learning the craft and learning how good writing works.

How You Read

Reading as a writer requires that you slow down and pay attention to the story as a story. It requires reading a passage, even an entire piece, more than once. The first time through, you can allow yourself to be caught up in the story (though the more you read as a writer, the tougher it becomes to let go completely of your consciousness of the piece as a piece, as something created by a writer). After you finish a piece that strikes you as successful in some way, go back and find out how the writer achieved that success.

As an editor at *Story* magazine, I read thousands of stories. These helped me improve tremendously as a writer. It was particularly helpful to read some stories from those authors we chose to publish many times. In selecting, editing, copyediting, and proofreading the stories for each issue, I read them more than a dozen times. The repetition helped me realize how the stories worked. I learned how the stories were structured and how the writers achieved certain effects. If you want to read as a writer, you have to be willing to read the same piece a number of times. As you read, try to place yourself in the writer's place. What ideas drive the piece? What possibilities exist within those ideas? Given those possibilities, what choices did the writer make? Why? What difficulties existed in making those ideas work on the page? What did the writer do to surmount those difficulties?

The more you read as a writer, the better you'll become. *Elements of the Writing Craft*, by Robert Olmstead, is a very good book on this subject, and I recommend it highly as a way of learning to read more insightfully as a writer. Olmstead breaks storytelling down to its smallest moves and provides examples from great writing to show those moves in action. If you want to learn how to read better as a writer, get a copy of this book.

Get copies of a lot of books. Begin reading them. Make time in your weekly schedule for reading. You'll find yourself improving more quickly as a writer, and you'll find yourself a much more insightful critic of your own work. If an idea isn't working, you'll know it—and why—more quickly than before.

Questions to Consider

1. How much do you read? How can you build time into your schedule for more reading?
2. What have you read in the past year that impressed you or moved you? What did the writer do to make you think or feel that way?
3. What writers are your favorites? What is it about their work that you particularly enjoy? Are there writers who were favorites at earlier times in your life that no longer appeal to you? Why have they lost their appeal?

Put It On Paper

PROMPT: Make a list of your top five pieces of published writing. Reread those five pieces, this time from the perspective of one writer learning from another. Make notes in the margins or in your notebook. Focus on the ideas that drive the piece and how the writer was able to execute those ideas on the page. What obstacles were overcome? How did the writer complicate and develop the ideas?

PROMPT: From the previous list, choose one piece and spend at least a week reading it a number of times. If it's a long piece, such as a novel, read a few chapters or a section. Each time you read it, make more notes. Again, practice reading as a writer. Assess what's working. Assess what you'd have done differently. Concentrate on discovering how the writer brought the main ideas to life.

PROMPT: Dig through your archives of writing and read something you wrote a long time ago. It might be a school report or a diary entry or a creative piece. After you recover from the glow (or the horror) of nostalgia, try to read it objectively. What ideas drive the piece? Can you read it objectively? If, at the time, you thought it was a fabulous piece, what do you think now? Can it be saved?

PROMPT: Steal an idea from something you've read. And not just a little idea. Steal the premise of a piece, its main conflict or situation. Write at least a page, shamelessly lifting this premise but changing names of characters, location, whatever. Then, after a page, add a complication of your own, one different from the first major complication in the piece. Write at least one more page.

PROMPT: Write a brief report about a piece you've written, but write the report from the point of view of an objective reader. Refer to "the writer" rather than to yourself. Assess what's working with the piece and what needs help. Consider what you, "the reviewer," would have done differently.

PROMPT: Keep an ongoing list of new words you learn while reading. Make this list a key part of your writer's notebook.

PROMPT: Keep an ongoing list of phrases and sentences that strike you as particularly good in what you read. Get into the habit of writing them down.

PROMPT: Steal a line from something you've read. It might only be a phrase, but grab that sucker and plunk it into a piece of your own. If you don't have a piece in progress, spend a session exploring an idea in which that line or phrase can appear.

PROMPT: Extend the story of a minor character or person in a piece you've read. Is there a character in a novel who intrigues you, who you wish played a larger role? Spend a session exploring that character's life, circumstances, or situation. James B. Hall took this approach in a story he wrote about Friday, the sidekick in Daniel Defoe's *Robinson Crusoe*. The title character does not appear in the story at all. It takes place after Crusoe has been rescued.

PROMPT: Read something in a form you usually don't read, and spend a session adding elements of that form to an on-going project—or you might try beginning a new project. For example, if you usually limit your reading to literary fiction, spend a couple of hours with a thriller or romance novel. As we've discussed, read as a writer, noting how stories in the form are told. What assumptions do they make of their readers? How are conflicts established? How are the characters presented?

Chapter Nine

Other People's Ideas

A fact of life: We can see with absolute clarity and know exactly the right course of action in other people's lives. Our own? That's another matter. The same is true for writing. We can see the flaws as well as the strengths in someone else's work, while our own work confuses us, makes us question our perceptions. The wrong turns are tougher to detect. The charms of a piece go unnoticed.

It doesn't take a great leap of logic, therefore, to realize that you can learn valuable lessons about assessing your own ideas by assessing those of other writers. In the previous chapter we discussed honing your critical skills by reading more and by learning to read with a writer's eye. In this chapter we'll look at how you can improve your skills at assessing your own ideas by evaluating the ideas of writers a bit closer to home.

In my workshops, we analyze the work of great writers, but often the gap in technical mastery between these masters and the students is so wide that the students can't quite grasp how to apply the technical devices in their own work. And it's tougher to imagine the masters struggling with developing an idea. Their classic work is so, well, classic that it seems to have dropped fully formed from their minds onto the page.

The work of fellow students, however, is much easier to assess. There's the genial older man, for example, who sits in the back and writes painfully sweet pieces of first-person nostalgia. His little gems glitter with charm, and yet lack narrative tension of any kind. They're made up of strung-together anecdotes that could appear in almost any order. As fellow writers, we can suggest ways of exploring his initial idea, pushing it to richer possibilities.

And then there's the silent woman whose every assigned piece ends up working through her recent divorce from a selfish, bullying s.o.b named John. Every piece she submits to the class is passionate, even riveting for a while, and yet finally is engulfed by a wave of rage. It's not difficult to see how the material is still too close to handle well in a literary context. It's easy to suggest that writing through her anger and grief could be done more productively in a journal or could be used to inform a piece on an unrelated subject. When she reads to us from a new story about gun-runners in South America—a nefarious group led by a selfish, bullying s.o.b. named Juan—we applaud her much firmer handle on the material that is infused with a passion that extends rather than dominates the tale.

Writers workshops and writers groups, therefore, offer invaluable experience in developing your critical skills and your ability to assess your ideas. Though applying your skills to your own work is more diffi-cult than applying them to the work of other writers, the practice will help you make the leap. You'll hone your skills so that it's easier to see unexplored possibilities as well as flaws in your work.

Response From Other Writers

The company of writers—whether in a group that meets regularly on an informal basis or one that gathers for a class or seminar—also can help you learn to assess your ideas by providing feedback on your work. You can gain a greater objectivity on your work by seeing it afresh through the eyes of others. You can develop a sense of your patterns as a writer when you hear similar comments on a variety of pieces. By understand-ing yourself more fully as a writer, you will more quickly realize the quality of your ideas and how they can be developed. The key: informed listening. Hear what your readers say. That's not always simple to do. It requires us to shed our sensitivity for a time, to put our fragile egos aside and listen, even when we don't want to hear that the story remains muddled or that we took a wrong turn on page six. Hearing your readers also is difficult because often your reader is working at a similar level of mastery and experience. She might sense instinctively that a character isn't working but cannot say why the character isn't working in a useful and accurate way.

To illustrate, let's extend the example of the woman writing the divorce story based on her own experience. The material she's using for her work is very close to her heart. She's sensitive about the situation and will be sensitive toward critical comments about work that explores the situation. To benefit from the comments of the class she needs to divorce herself (pardon the pun) from the real-life events that inspired the piece. The story that exists is the one that's on the page. Openness and objectivity are essential.

The example is based on a woman in one of my workshops. She wrote a narrative (autobiographical fiction) about her divorce and several members of the class commented (quite astutely) that the husband in the story was one-dimensional. Every time he appeared he said the same type of cruel, passive-aggressive comments. The writer grinned at us and shrugged. She said the character was based on her ex-husband, who was a one-dimensional person. The writer felt this was a valid defense of her story, but she was wrong. Her feelings toward the ex-husband blinded her to the limitations of the character on the page. If the guy truly was one-dimensional in real life, then he's not a good source for a fictional character.

In our groups and workshops, we also have to listen between the lines. Even when we can get beyond our personal connection to the piece and view it more objectively, we may not be able to discern the nature of a problem. Our fellow apprentice writers will tend to point to symptoms and recommend a quick fix rather than be able to see deeper into concerns. Sometimes they can sense a problem but can't articulate it or recommend a useful solution. In the previous example, the members complained that the husband was predictable and uninteresting.

Their suggestion: Have him do something different, something less predictable. The real issue, however, is the writer's relationship to the material. She needs distance on the husband character. By arbitrarily including a detail or action to broaden the character, she hasn't solved the problem. Now a flat, predictable character simply has become less predictable. The writer doesn't see him in a fresh way. He's still the dreaded *Ex*, just a bit more concealed now.

If the writer listens between the lines, she'll hear that the husband character isn't working. She'll step back and assess the possibilities. Perhaps she needs to change the character in a significant way in her mind and imagination. Cut as many ties as possible with the real-life model for the character. Explore the possibilities of a strikingly new character, whose actions will create new and richer possibilities for the story.

Listening between the lines also will help you sort through the array of contradictory comments that your fellow workshoppers might provide. You've probably had the experience of submitting a story for comments only to hear that five people think it's perfect, three enjoyed it but didn't like the ending, and two love the ending but felt the middle lacked tension. What to do?

Again: listen between the lines. What patterns can you find in the comments? Why does the middle seem to lack tension? Have you strayed from the story's essential conflict, perhaps by introducing a new situation? And has that new situation created new expectations for your reader, ones that are not resolved by the ending? Furthermore, how do these concerns fit comments you've heard regarding your previously submitted stories? Do your readers often say they find your endings unsatisfying? If so, review your stories and find out if you're setting up expectations early on that don't fit your true goals. Do your readers lavish praise on your early pages but note that the middle pages lag? Perhaps you need to complicate the initial idea with more ideas sooner than you thought.

The point is that contradictory advice might be less contradictory if you explore the roots of the concerns rather than the surface symptoms.

And by treating the roots, you'll gain a better understanding of the piece and of yourself as a writer. Moreover, apprentice writers can provide valuable feedback on concerns, but their advice on remedies will be less informed. For that type of advice, you need to work on the story, gain a better understanding of the concerns, and then take your own advice.

If you're in a workshop, rather than in a group of writer/friends who are working at approximately the same level of mastery, seek help from the instructor. The instructor's advice can help you hone your skills at assessing your work by offering more useful solutions to problems in a particular piece. Some instructors will be more helpful than others, of course. They'll understand our goals as writers and the demands of the material we're exploring. But it's important to work with more than one instructor as you develop your craft. Even those who are less simpatico with us can increase our understanding of our work and our ideas.

Though there is no formula for assessing our ideas and the way those ideas are manifest on the page, using the work of other writers, and listening to the comments of other writers on our work can help us develop a critical aesthetic, which we can use to make more informed decisions about our ideas. Don't discount what you can learn from other writers. Use what you learn to make yourself a better editor of your own work, a better evaluator of it. The decisions you make are, in the end, your own.

 ## Questions to Consider

1. Do you meet regularly with other writers to respond to each other's work? If so, how useful are the comments you receive? How can you make the experience more useful?

2. Can you hear comments on your work objectively? If not, why not? How can you make yourself less sensitive and, thereby, more objective?

3. Do other writers consider you an insightful reader of their work? If so, how can you more fully apply this skill to your own work? What makes you a good reader?

4. What patterns exist in the comments you've received about your work? What can they teach you about yourself as a writer? How can they help you more effectively assess your ideas?

Put It On Paper

P R O M P T : Write a short piece about the best writing advice you ever received, advice that allowed you to see your work in a new way or advice that was especially inspiring. How did you hear the advice? Who gave it? What changes did it prompt in your work? How did it help you understand yourself better as a writer?

P R O M P T : Review a piece that has been critiqued by someone else. It might be a piece you submitted to a class, your writers group, or simply to a friend. Write a response to the critique, focusing on what it tells you about the piece and about yourself as a writer. If you want to be defensive and petulant, arguing against the critique, go ahead, but at some point try to evaluate the critique dispassionately. Even if you feel that most of the comments are way off the mark, which ones seem valuable? Try to listen between the lines, as we discussed earlier in this chapter. What is being said *without* being said? How does the critique fit other comments you've received on your work?

P R O M P T : Write a page-long critique of a piece you wrote awhile ago, trying to view it as someone else's work. Focus on the ideas, how they're presented and developed. Do you find undeveloped possibilities for the piece? What are the strengths and weaknesses in the piece? How does it compare to more recent work you've done? Are similar characters and themes and ideas being explored?

PROMPT: Spend some time reading your work, from a fully realized piece to fragments and false starts. Write a page or so about this writer's body of work from a third-person perspective. What themes and ideas appear regularly? What are the writer's strengths and weaknesses? How are the ideas developed and explored?

PROMPT: Write a page-long critique of another writer's work, preferably an unpublished piece, a work in progress. Focus on the ideas, how they're presented and developed. Be as candid as possible—and as objective! Sometimes in classes and groups we treat a piece too kindly, hoping not to hurt the writer's feelings or hoping that the writer will treat our work with equal kindness. Here's your chance to be brutally honest.

PROMPT: Write a page about what you learned by doing the previous prompt, the critique of another writer's work. How did that critique develop your understanding of your own work, your tastes and beliefs.

PROMPT: Write about advice you received but rejected. Why did you reject it? Would you reject it today or can you see some value in it?

PROMPT: Spend a session writing a piece that focuses on putting into practice some advice you've received from a teacher or from another writer. For example, if someone whose opinion you respect has noted that you have a tendency to present unnecessarily lavish or detailed descriptions of setting, write a scene in which such descriptions are shorter and more useful. The advice may be true, partly true, or not true at all, but putting it into practice can help you decide if it's worth remembering or not. It's also worth exploring a tendency or pattern that a respected reader notices. Perhaps the pattern is simply an aspect of your writing style, or, on the other hand, perhaps you should explore other approaches now and again.

PROMPT: Let's reverse the previous prompt. Spend a session writing a piece that flies in the face of advice you've received. If you've been told that your endings tend to be sentimental, pour on the sentiment. Your ending should be so sweet your reader gains five pounds reading it. The point is not to ignore the advice. It might be valid and worth noting. Taking time to examine it—even in such a stubborn way—is worth doing. If the advice is something that might hold you back, then flying in the face of it is a good idea too.

PROMPT: Spend a session changing the ending of another writer's work. The ending, as written by the other writer might be fine but simply not the way you would have done it. Write it the way *you* would write it. If this exercise interests you, take a session to do the opposite. Rewrite one of your own endings the way another writer might have done it. How would Joyce Carol Oates, for example, have ended your recently finished short story? Of course, you have to choose a writer whose style and sensibility you know well.

Chapter Ten

Gaining Distance

The cliché about hindsight being 20/20 hangs around because there's a lot of truth in it. We look back on decisions we made five, ten, twenty years ago and can see with often rueful clarity the errors we made. If you've been writing awhile, you've had a similar experience with your work, I'm sure. Oh, the sweet pain of reading that story from college, the one we were sure would soon turn us into the literary scene's next Young Turk. It so clearly embodied our poetic souls, put forth such a sad yet triumphant lyricism that it would bring readers to tears throughout the world. When we read it now, however, it sounds like the pretentious gibberish of the ambitious sophomore who wrote it.

Unfortunately, that distance gained by years is difficult to achieve in other ways, but unless you are content to finish a piece every decade or two you'll have to find some ways to help you gain a clear perspective on your work, clear enough to make the necessary assessments. Assessing your ideas—in their most raw form as well as in their more polished ones—requires a level of objectivity. The closer you are to the material emotionally and psychologically, the more distance you need to create in order to see clearly and assess the piece. An idea that moves you profoundly is worth investigating in a piece of writing, but it may require more refined ideas to make it come alive for the reader. You could be deeply moved while writing an early draft and believe it has a power that is not yet on the page.

A case in point: In graduate school I went to a reading by a respected writer who had published several collections of short stories. He read a long story that he'd written recently. (Our most recent work tends to be our favorite work.) The story was—at the risk of being unkind— excruciatingly dull. One person, a teacher in the program, even fell asleep, jerking awake with a loud bang of his foot against the back of the seat in front of him. And yet, as the story reached its climax, the writer began to fight back tears. His throat closed, and he had to pause for a few seconds before reading the ending. By that point most of us had lost the thread of the story, and we were aghast that what seemed to be an uninspired tale held such power for the writer.

The story in his mind was not yet on the page. From what I recall, there seemed to be some autobiographical threads running through the story. The writer was responding to those personal memories. He needed more distance from the material to notice that the story, though deeply moving to him, was not yet moving to others.

Strategies to Gain Distance

Seasoned writers develop their own methods of gaining the distance necessary to effectively assess their ideas. My favorite is one I heard years ago from a professor, though I've never been able to validate. The professor told us that a bestselling author found that he couldn't see a piece with fresh eyes until it appeared in print, especially in a glossy magazine. Something about the shiny paper, I don't know. He would consider a piece finished, then send it to his editor. When he read the published version, he saw all the wrong turns and missed opportunities, as well as the less-than-perfect phrasings. And so the author would type a draft, then tack it to a corkboard hanging on a wall in his office. He hung a wall light with a bendable neck above the corkboard, positioning the light to shine directly onto the tacked pages. He then walked to the other side of his office and read the piece through binoculars. The glare of the light simulated glossy pages, and he gained the distance he needed to assess the piece.

I'm not recommending this approach. I'm simply showing the lengths to which authors will go to objectify a piece in process, so that they can see it anew. Without that freshness of perspective, it's tough to assess what's going well and what needs help.

From my own experience, I do read a piece differently when the published version arrives in the mail or in the bookstore. It does always seem a bit different from the version grown so familiar on the computer screen. Once I even cursed the magazine editor who obviously had re-written entire passages, substituting a number of awkward phrases and clunky transitions for my crystalline prose. The nerve! I rushed to my computer to gather evidence to cite in the vitriolic letter already taking shape in my mind. Other than a word or two and some minor punctuation, she hadn't changed anything. The clunkers, alas, were my own.

Other times I've seen places that might have been more fully developed, thought of ideas that seemed so obvious and yet hadn't occurred to me. I don't know that it's a matter of the glossy paper so much as the distance between the time the piece is submitted and its final publication. It's also the writer's mindset. When you read your published work you read it through the eyes of all the readers who will find it in the magazine or the book. They provide a wonderfully useful (and sometimes heartbreaking) distance that's tough to conjure on our own.

I had a writing professor who typed (this is going back some years) on three typewriters, using one for the first stage of the work, a second for the next stage, and so on. Each typewriter had a different color ribbon. This approach worked for him, helping him see the piece with fresh eyes. It also helped him relax and explore on the first typewriter. He knew that on the second or third typewriter he could change something that wasn't quite right.

Such strategies work for you or they don't. Experiment. The most common advice on the matter is to file a piece and move to something else for a while. Sometimes a few weeks or a month is all you need to gain the right distance. Meanwhile, the piece percolates, consciously as well as unconsciously. You think of new ideas or ways to refine earlier ideas. However, as I said in an earlier chapter, when you put away a piece, give yourself a time limit. That way it won't be left untouched for so long that it loses its pull on your imagination. All writers have too many fragments in their files, half-written pieces that have been filed as "failures" or ones to which we hesitate to return, thinking that someday we will, but these pieces languish beyond the time when we actually can return.

Yet another strategy for gaining the necessary distance is to change the time when you write or the place where you write. If you write early in the morning, before heading for work or school, make time in the evening to read the work in progress. Or if you write in the evenings, read your piece in the morning, before heading out for the day. We tend to be in different emotional, mental, and psychological states at different times of the day. Many writers are sharper in the morning but a bit more regimented too. In the dreamy glow of evening, their minds are looser, more adventuresome. Reading a piece in progress at an unusual time of day can provide some objectivity. Do the ideas still work? Does the new mindset provide new inspirations?

Reading in a different place from where you write also can help. If possible, get out of your living space. Go to a library or coffee house or to a park. You'll find that you'll see the piece differently. Your awareness of different surroundings adds a fresh element to your conscious mind, altering the way you perceive what you're reading. You'll understand the piece in a new way.

Yet another method is to send it to a trusted reader. This approach gets the piece out of your hands for a while, which is good, especially when you're feeling stuck or indecisive or have begun to lose faith in your idea. You also may find that by giving it to the reader you are able to see the piece through his or her perspective even before you receive any comments. You gain a new sense of what's working.

The Imaginary Reader

To explore that point a bit, you might want to imagine giving it to a reader. In other words, read the piece yourself but conjure if you can that reader's viewpoint. How would she or he see the piece? What would make her laugh? What would surprise and delight him? In the previous chapter I mentioned paying attention to the comments of a writing instructor. Often a gifted instructor's ideas will stay with us throughout our lives, will help to shape our own critical aesthetic. If you have the good fortune of working with a gifted instructor, imagine sending the piece to him or her.

I advise you not to actually give a piece to a reader until you have it well underway. If you're simply looking for some validation on a raw idea, it's better to work through the idea first. You might detect a note of doubt in your reader's voice, causing you to doubt the idea in a significant way and quickly abandon it, when the reader's doubt might be imagined or might result from the idea needing refinement rather than abandonment. If the reader loves the idea, you might feel inspired to continue or you might have received your reward for it and lose your desire to continue to develop it. You may not realize either of these feelings on a conscious level, but they still can be there—and they're dangerous to a work in the early stages. Save your trusted reader for something more developed. Imagining your reader's comments might be enough to give you some distance.

Consider reading the piece aloud. You should read your work aloud when you're in the proofing and editing stage, but try reading it even in first-draft form, even if certain sections are still not finished. How does it sound to you? Where do the ideas need to be stronger, and which ones are working well? Some writers tell me they can't stand to hear their voices on tape, but if you can stand it, tape record yourself reading the piece aloud. Then you can sit back and have it read to you and hear it in a fresh way. It won't seem so close to you. Or, if you're really brave, ask someone you trust to read it to you. Their voices won't give the piece the same inflections and emphasis that you would give it, but that's okay. Sometimes we supply emphasis that isn't there. And at this stage we're simply trying to assess the ideas and the ways they've been executed on the page. It doesn't matter if the character cries out "I *love* you" or "I love *you*."

Questions to Consider

1. Before assessing the work in progress, have you created enough distance to see it clearly, or at least as clearly as possible? Do you tend to reject your ideas too quickly? Do you stick with them for too long?

2. Have you given a piece enough time in the drawer so that you can see it? Is it time to read it again or to revisit an idea that remains half-formed?

3. When you've found a way to create enough distance to assess your ideas as they are manifest on the page, ask yourself the basic questions first: How meaningful is this idea, and, therefore, this project? Is the idea merely clever or has it yielded greater and varied depths? Does the idea deliver its basic goal? By that I mean, if the idea is essentially comic, has it led to a funny or entertaining draft? If the idea is essentially a melancholy reflection, does the piece that embodies it evoke that tone and those emotions? If so, what new ideas will take the piece even further in that direction? If not, what's missing? Are there flaws in the executions holding back the idea, or does the idea seem to want to go in a new direction?

4. The final question in number three deserves further development. Sometimes the generative spark, the first idea, is simply a way into material that might be quite different from what you expect. Does the draft, for example, lack humor, despite the comic nature of the initial idea, because the humor was leading you to darker material than you anticipated?

Put It On Paper

PROMPT: Though the conventional wisdom tells us to try to forget about a draft while it's gestating, odds are it's going to surface in your mind from time to time. You'll think of a new idea—a fresh stanza, a line of dialogue, a description of a place. Take time to write these ideas on paper and put them in the file with the draft. Feel free to forget about them afterward. When you pull the draft from hibernation, you'll discover any number of little scraps of paper with ideas for developing the piece, ideas you may have forgotten entirely.

PROMPT: Change the time when you write for the next few sessions. As we discussed earlier in the chapter, the change in time will produce a change in mindset, allowing you to assess your ideas from a fresh perspective.

PROMPT: Change the place where you write for the next few sessions. The shift in geography can supply a fresh perspective.

PROMPT: Spend a writing session rooting through old files and note-books. It's probably been years since you looked at some of what you've written. Use that distance to reevaluate abandoned projects. Look for patterns among the ideas. Look for ideas that can be moved from stalled projects and to ongoing ones.

PROMPT: If you've taken time to do the previous prompt, choose one idea from your files that appeals to you and make it the focus of your next writing session. Explore and develop the idea, bringing to it all you've learned since the time you first put that one on paper.

PROMPT: Extending the previous two prompts, write a page or two in which you respond to what you've discovered in your cache of earlier ideas, fragments, and drafts. What patterns run through the work? What themes run through the work? What do these fragments suggest about you as a writer—your interests and inspirations?

PROMPT: Shift the distance you feel from the piece by reading it as if it were someone else's story. This shift may be difficult, but give it a try. Imagine that you discovered the piece in a magazine or a book. From this perspective, does the piece work? What advice would you offer this writer in revising the piece?

PROMPT: Spend a session recasting the piece in a new point of view. If it's a first-person piece, shift to third, for example. You need do this only for the first few pages. Has your perspective changed? Can you read it with fresh eyes?

PROMPT: Read the piece as if you plan to burn it as soon as you finish reading it. No other person will ever read the piece. You need not be concerned, therefore, with the glory and fame the piece will bring you. You need not squirm at the thought that the piece reveals some slightly unsavory thoughts. You need not please or displease anyone else with the piece. Seen in that light, what do you want to change? What do you want to keep at all costs? Does the piece please you? Was it worth writing despite the fact that no one but you will ever read it? Would you have written it knowing no one will ever read it?

Chapter Eleven

Letting Go

After a recent workshop, a student told me, "The only time I can really think of ideas is when I'm not trying to think of ideas. As soon as you tell us to 'brainstorm' my brain shuts down." She was exaggerating her claim—in fact, she produced some excellent ideas in the workshop—but there's an element of truth in her statement. We can force ourselves to write and to assess and develop our ideas, to the point where we kill any fun or creativity that might help make the ideas better. We put pressure on ourselves, blocking ourselves from thinking by repeating a silent mantra of "Think, think, think."

In the past few chapters, we've focused on an analytical approach—learning techniques from other writers, practicing our techniques on the work of other writers, creating distance to see and analyze our work in progress. In this chapter, we'll explore the other side of that approach, one based on intuition, stillness, listening to what the piece is trying to tell us.

As we've discussed, writing is an intuitive process. It doesn't submit to formulas or guidelines. It requires, instead, a level of faith on the part of the writer, using her craft to give shape to the ideas while also allowing them to take their own shapes. That approach goes against the way we try to order our lives. To keep up with bills or get the kids to activities on time, to remain efficient and productive at our jobs, we make lists to follow. We prioritize. We work to keep things under control. It's tough, therefore, to let go when it's time to write. Though writing is a form of escape from the details and necessities of our more practical lives, too often we don't allow ourselves to escape. We structure our days to allow for an hour to write, a sacrifice that makes us demand production from that hour. We've got to have something to show for it.

This approach can make us reject our ideas too quickly. We think of an idea, burn with it for a while, writing furiously over the course of days or weeks. But when we feel the first surge of disappointment that our idea on the page doesn't look like the idea in our minds, we declare it "stupid" or "unworkable" and ditch it. Spending more time on it, we think, would simply be a waste. Or, we ride our initial inspiration by trying to rein in the idea, to capture and control it on the page. We know what the piece is supposed to be, and, by gum, we're going to make it exactly that.

Evaluating

When evaluating your ideas as they're manifest on the page, the first step is to assess without labeling. Your goal is not to declare what's "good" or "bad." You're trying to discover the nature of the idea. When you begin exploring your ideas on paper, you're figuring out what it is. What's the story here? What clues are appearing within the descriptions or the characters? How is the material manifesting itself? Which characters are moving in directions you didn't foresee? Which ideas spark still more ideas? What shape seems to be emerging from the piece? What new possibilities occur to you as you read and reread?

The process of assessing ideas should be creative. It should inspire ideas as much as sort through them. You are trying to find the hidden nature of your idea rather than judging whether it's worthy of further pursuit. You are not shutting down your creative self; you're opening it. Your first passes through the draft should be ones of discovery. Focus on what's on the page rather than bemoaning what's not yet there.

In her essay "Lost in the Woods," Cathy Ann Johnson compares the creative process to wandering in the woods:

There is an art to wandering. If I have a destination, a plan—an objective—I've lost my ability to find serendipity. I've become too focused, too single-minded. I am on a quest, not a ramble. I search for the Holy Grail of particularity and miss the chalice freely offered, filled full and overflowing.

There are times when I go to the woods to find specific wild-flowers or plants or animals, to illustrate an article or a book, armed with sketchpad and pencils. At those times I set my inner viewfinder for plants, or animals, or whatever—and my larger vision is as limited as if I were looking through the wrong end of a telescope. I've preconceived a notion and closed my mind and my eyes to whatever else may be offered free, gratis.

Many of us manage to conjure Johnson's process of wandering in the very early stages of a project, but when it's time to step back and see what we've done, we grab that "wrong end of a telescope." Instead, as we move deeper into a project, we can put to use the critical skills discussed in the previous few chapters by allowing those skills to inform an open-minded reading. As we assess a project, we'll make better decisions if we keep our minds open than if we limit ourselves by taking on a "quest" mentality.

That mentality hampers your vision, and it can stall the project that began with such great promise. One of my favorite pieces about the process of writing is the film *Barton Fink*. If you haven't seen it, treat yourself. It's brilliant on many levels, but let's discuss it from a writer's view. As you may know, Barton is a successful playwright in pre-World War II America. He writes about, as he loves to say, "the common man." And yet he grudgingly leaves Broadway to write in Hollywood, where he hopes to make a lot of money. The studio assigns him "a wrestling picture." Throughout much of the movie, we see him struggle with the project, barely writing any words at all. He is stalled by his desire to please his Hollywood bosses, despite the fact that he knows next to nothing about the form. Though he spouts passionately about his love for the common man, he knows little about the common man's reality. And he's too busy spouting to realize that his neighbor, a beefy insurance salesman named Charlie Meadows, is a potential fount of stories and is eager to tell them. At the climax of the film, Charlie gets to the heart of Barton's problem when he roars, "You. Don't. Listen."

Joel and Ethan Coen, the writers of the film, were struggling with a different screenplay when they began writing *Barton Fink*, and I wonder if the admonition about listening was targeted in some ways at themselves. We're all guilty of not listening from time to time. The idea Barton struggles to find is right in front of him, but he doesn't hear it. As you move through your draft, take time to listen. Free it from the expectations of some vague and fickle audience. Free it from your own hopes that it will verify your creative genius to the world.

If you feel the piece is not working, ask yourself if those expectations are blinding you or making you deaf to the more authentic idea contained within the one you're struggling to develop. Or, perhaps, the idea lacks vitality because it's dishonest from the start, is a way of cashing in on commercial trends or a way of eliciting praise from your writers group or workshop. It's not dishonest, of course, to write commercially, but understand that that's what you're doing and find the place inside you that's invested more deeply in the project. Even the most commercial writers have to believe in the efficacy of their work at some level.

Or, perhaps, the idea is working better than you think, but you're pressuring it to be something that it's not, for the reasons mentioned above. Or, perhaps, the idea is growing larger and, in some ways, messier than you expected when you began developing it. For some writers, this would be good news: "I thought I'd caught a little fish, but the weight on my line shows I've hooked a much bigger one!" For other writers, the hard and heavy tug on the line is scary. What monster of the deep have we accidentally hooked? They cut the line in fear they'll lose their line, rod, and boat.

The key, of course, is listening.

Informed Listening

You might be wondering why we discussed developing and honing critical skills in the opening chapters of this section if the evaluation process is so passive. Good question. The answer is that you're not passively listening. You're actively listening. Compare it to the process of meditation. In a meditative state we are, ideally, both relaxed and alert. We lose ourselves by being utterly conscious of the moment. We empty ourselves in order to fill ourselves.

When evaluating your work, try to find a similar balance. Your critical skills will inform your listening. The more you develop the critical skills the less you will need to be aware of them in a conscious way. You have read the masters. You have studied your genre. You have taken part in workshops or writers groups, learning from writers at your own level. You have listened to experienced writers critique submissions. You have worked hard at your craft. With the skills you develop in your training you can *listen* to your drafts in an informed way. The confidence you gain through hard work will help you to let go and allow your ideas to be what they want to be. You can trust yourself to let go. The skills you've learned will be there, even as you open yourself to all possibilities.

Evaluating ideas, therefore, requires a balance of critical skills and passive openness. As you read your draft, be alert to possibilities. Read and reread. Then read it again. What patterns emerge? What do these patterns seem to suggest about the piece? How might the patterns be explored more fully?

While reading, be mindful of where you trip. If you tend to trip at the same spot whenever you take a pass, make a quick mark in the margin. Ask yourself why this idea or phrase or image stops you. Is it not organic to the piece? Perhaps it needs to be cut or perhaps it's trying to assert itself more fully into the story.

As the piece develops through successive drafts, keep asking these questions and keep your mind both relaxed and alert. As the piece continues to develop, it will be clear which ideas don't fit, which ones are redundant, which ones belong elsewhere, perhaps even in a different piece. It will be clear if a line in a poem or a scene in a short story is not working, because those around it now are working. It also will be clear which details are relics of an earlier draft and no longer fit the piece, because now you have a better understanding of where you are going.

You can use this method from the first tickle of inspiration through the final draft, developing some ideas, discarding others, seeing all the stages in the process as equally creative, ones that require a balance between the critical skills you've developed and an openness to possibility and discovery. As you listen, be mindful of destructive or distracting self-talk: "This is stupid, because I'm a lousy writer." "This will be a failure like all the other things I've written." "This is great because I am a genius!" "Readers are going to weep in their chairs when they read that line!" "Is this idea great or lousy? Am I just wasting my time, or is this idea worth pursuing?" "This is going to be good, damn it, I don't care what it takes."

Those statements create noise that makes it difficult to hear the piece in progress. They have nothing to do with what's on the page. They're symptoms of the insecurity and grandiosity we all share. They profess faith in an empirical grid of "good" and "bad." They upset the balance we've discussed in this chapter. When you're listening as you read, you'll hear these thoughts. They may even try to take over. Recognize them and push them aside. They're not on the page, and they're really not even about what's on the page. They are born of fear—of failing, of succeeding, of hard work, of committing to a long project, of exploring emotions and ideas we'd rather not face. Keep your focus on the page. Keep your ears open to the ideas and the words on the page. The other stuff doesn't matter. It's simply you trying to get in your own way. Instead, like Cathy Johnson, wander in the woods and be open to what is there for free.

Questions to Consider

1. As you assess and evaluate your ideas, are you listening to what's on the page, rather than trying too hard to control the piece? Are you seeking to balance passivity and activity? Critical skills with stillness?

2. Can you avoid labeling your ideas, looking instead at their potential, their appropriateness, at what they're trying to tell you?

3. Do you subconsciously determine that the early stage of writing is *creative* and the later stages *evaluative*? If so, how might you sustain a balance between these modes of perception throughout the process of writing?

4. Do you clutter your mind with concerns about how this draft reflects on you—I'm a genius! I'm a loser!—rather than focusing on the piece itself? How can you use your awareness of this tendency to keep it from distracting you from the more authentic needs of your writing projects?

Put It On Paper

PROMPT: As you assess a piece in progress, underline the main ideas—the primary conflict, plot, emotions, characters, themes. Rather than labeling them or assessing if they're "good" or "bad," write each at the top of a blank page, then brainstorm any possibilities that spring to mind, even if they don't seem to be related. Put the "storms" aside for a day, then read them, noting which ones draw you in most. Use these ideas as the basis for at least a page of writing.

PROMPT: Return to a piece you've abandoned and read it with the balanced listening approach we've discussed in this chapter. Circle or highlight the lines, phrases, images or anything in the piece that grabs you in some way. Read the piece again, this time focusing only on the highlighted passages. Is there a pattern running through them? An image motif? A character? A thread of action? Now read the sections that aren't highlighted. Is there a pattern here too? Explore the pattern of the highlighted passages. How can it be developed? What might be discarded from the sections that didn't engage you?

PROMPT: Expanding on the previous prompt, write one of the high-lighted passages at the top of a page and begin exploring it as a separate entity rather than as part of the work in progress. Allow yourself to create new ideas around it, knowing that you can return it to its original home later. For now, see what else it might reveal.

PROMPT: Write down all the destructive and distracting self-talk state-ments you usually make while evaluating your work—all the statements you use to create noise and thereby deafen yourself to the piece in progress. Now read the piece and immediately discard any thoughts that your list contains.

Chapter Twelve

Ideas for
Another Time

When I was a reporter I covered a few school board meetings where a certain parent regularly showed up to excoriate the board members about some grievance or other. His arguments always had a certain idealistic validity but were so convoluted, impractical, and emotional that most people at the meeting rolled their eyes and ignored him. He was a wild-looking guy—long gray hair, stoop-shouldered, intense blue eyes. As he spoke, his voice rose to a stentorian pitch, then sometimes broke into a parrot screech. He was a wanna-be lawyer and loved to sling legal jargon at the board members, who he felt were oppressing him somehow. Given that the city I covered was a bland, middle-class bedroom community, I welcomed his intrusions. He made the meetings much more interesting.

I wrote a news story about him, getting to know him better. He was a paradoxical guy, as obnoxious as he was smart, as belligerent as he was sad, as selfish and egomaniacal as he was generous and broken. Of course, I *had* to write a short story about him. So I tried. And tried. Yeah, pretty much tried again and again and again. It's been fifteen years since that time, and I have a file folder packed with drafts of that story. I tried a half-dozen points of view and at least that many structures. I changed beginnings and endings many times and worked the scenes as well as I knew how. I even plopped him into a completely different story for a while in hopes that by taking him fully out of any real-life context he might spring to life as a literary creation. Try as I might, I couldn't get him to yield to the page. Every now and again, I pluck that story from the filing cabinet and read it. There are moments in it that work well. But I decide every time that it's simply one that got away.

As writers, we need to face that decision sometimes. For a variety of reasons, an idea ends up not quite working. It may be a large idea—for a book-length project or a screenplay. It might be for a smaller piece. It might even be an idea for a character or a situation within a piece. At some point, we have to let go. Smaller ones, of course, are easier to give up. A sixty-page start on a stalled novel is a lot tougher to put aside.

Warning Signs

So how do you know if an idea doesn't work? Naturally, there's no rule-of-thumb, step-by-step formula for answering that question. However, there are discernible warning signs that an idea is in trouble.

Successive Drafts Don't Help

Sometimes an idea isn't bad at all, but it resists our attempts to develop it. As we've discussed, listening to the idea can help. It may be resisting because it doesn't want to follow our prescriptions for what it needs to be. It wants to be something different, and it's up to us to figure out the nature of the idea. But despite draft after draft and days and weeks and months of work, the idea isn't working. It isn't even getting clearer in our minds. It may be time to let go.

For example, a writer wants to write about a family picnic, held many years ago, that speaks to the nature of her childhood. Images of the event have been seeping into her mind, half-remembered comments, the geranium-colored dress her mother wore and the startling look of sadness in her eyes when, briefly, she took off her sunglasses. The writer begins writing about everything she can remember, trying to capture the mixture of innocence and melancholy, the joy of a sunny summer day in childhood and the inkling that life has less carefree days in store for us. But on the page the event feels pedestrian, anecdotal. Who cares about any of this stuff? The writer adds new dramatic elements, turning the memoir into fiction in hopes of energizing the piece while capturing a deeper truth. With those changes, however, she drifts further away from her initial vision. Now there arc moments bordering on melodrama. There's a strain, a false note running through the piece that's tough to pinpoint. She switches points of view, changes characters and actions. She tries a lighter tone, then a darker one. She introduces an entirely new context for the event. She brings it to her writers group, hoping for some insight. She puts it away for a month, but upon returning, her sense of the piece is even more remote. It seems wooden and self-conscious, and she can't quite grasp the feeling that inspired her to develop the idea in the first place.

As writers, we hear that genius is mostly a matter of hard work, and that's true. But this writer can make herself crazy trying to develop this idea, or she can admit that, at least for now, it's not going to happen. Continued work, rather than shedding light, seems to move the piece further away from its possibilities.

Enthusiasm Wanes

Sometimes we come up with an idea that seems great, especially to anyone we tell about it. We convulse people at parties with the story about our uncle Dave and his bizarre kleptomania. "You've got to put him in a story," people tell you time and again. And so you try, giggling away at the keyboard, the sounds of a laughing reader inspiring you forward. But as the story develops, it rings false. Uncle Dave, transferred to the page, refuses to be funny. Instead, he seems dull, even a bit tragic. As we work on the piece, we find ourselves less and less interested in it. We return to the piece with a sense of duty, with the belief that other people have found this a funny tale, but our hearts and minds aren't truly engaged. It may be time to let go, to let Uncle Dave continue to be a party favorite.

You'll know when you reach the point of diminishing returns, when the piece is no longer a struggle and has become a forced march, one for which you have no passion, not even anger. It has become a bore, and until you find a way to muster new energy for it, continuing is hopeless.

I suffered this problem recently while trying to write an essay about a runaway cow in my hometown of Cincinnati. I tried to use the cow as a foil for a deeper essay about the national recession and my own little piece of it. People in the city spoke often of the cow, and it became a national story. Friends from other parts of the country said they loved hearing about the cow on the news. So I wrote and wrote and wrote some more, using the cow situation as metaphor. But the essay never came together. I realized I was forcing myself to follow the cow story and had to admit that, deep down, I didn't care a damn about that cow.

A Growing Sense of Disconnection

Thoreau warned us many years ago about undertaking enterprises that require "new clothes." He meant, of course, we should avoid situations that insist we become someone we are not, that force us to be untrue to ourselves. Some ideas require the same approach. We set out with motives that are not tied to the idea itself. We want to sound wise on the page, to be admired by readers, to look hip or scholarly or empathic or any of a hundred things. Often we're not conscious of this desire. We feel we're burning to write about a subject, but what's really burning is our desire to appear to be a certain way. As we develop the project, we find it moving further away from who we are. The material continues to distance itself. Our words on the page ring false. The ideas themselves grow vague and indistinct. And we find ourselves, more and more, bluffing our way through.

If you find yourself in this situation, you may need to let go of the idea. It may be right for someone, but it's not right for you. The situation is common in the early stages of apprenticeship, when we try on various identities, speak in various voices. In college, I loved the work of F. Scott Fitzgerald and tried to mimic his long, lyrical sentences, and I tried to put his lush cadences on the page. Unfortunately, I also tried to write about what he wrote about. As a 20-year-old college student in the Midwest, I knew nothing about being an alcoholic writer in Hollywood coping with an institutionalized wife and fading memories of a glorious past. But I wrote a few stories about such characters. The stories were terrible. And

I suffered many false starts. I wondered what was wrong. Why did the ideas always seem so stupid when I put them on the page? When I conceived the ideas they seemed great, worthy of F. Scott himself. The answer to my questions lay in the material itself. When I began to write about a less literary world, one far less glamorous but one that was mine, a world I understood instinctively, I suffered fewer false starts. I was no longer bluffing.

Endless Beginnings

Earlier we discussed how the generative idea might simply be the conduit that leads us to the truly inspired idea. We must have faith and move forward, allowing the idea to evolve. However, sometimes we find ourselves shifting from one idea to the next in an endless series of discoveries. These discoveries change the piece in significant ways. Unfortunately, they don't lead to progressive development. They lead to our starting over in an endless chain of new beginnings.

If you find yourself in this situation, it may be time to let go. After a while, the nature of the core idea should reveal itself. If it doesn't do that, you don't fully understand the nature of the idea and may need to give it a rest, at least for a while. A friend of mine worked on a novel over the course of years. Every few months she'd update me on the project, and each time it sounded completely different from the time before. A minor character would emerge to take the novel in a new direction. Instead of a dark study of one subject, it would become a campy look at another subject. The next update would bring new subjects and treatments, a new protagonist. I couldn't help feeling that it was time for her to let go of the project, which had become an aimless amalgam of false starts. The more she invested her time and energy in the project, the higher the personal stake in the project rose. The finished piece gathered a greater and greater need to be, well, great. A project that had started with an engaging premise had evolved into a magnum opus that absolutely needed to set the literary world on its ear.

When you realize you're caught in a similar web, step back and consider your motives and approach. Have you invested too much personally in the piece to see it clearly? Are you trying to force new layers upon an idea that, for whatever reason, doesn't contain such layers? Is it time to let go of such endless work?

Honoring the Ideas That Don't Work

We've discussed avoiding labels for your ideas, and we've discussed ways to revive ideas and ways to strip away what's not working to save ideas. But sometimes an idea just isn't going to work. Though de-clutter experts would chide me for saying so, I advise you *not* to throw your idea away. I've heard a number of writers tell me how one night they realized their story or poem or novel wasn't working, and so they burned the pages in some ceremonial way. The organizational gurus would applaud such an act—a ritual cleansing! A symbol of your letting go of the project and of the past! A rite of passage that allows you to move on! Yes, these opinions are not without validity, and such symbolic acts might be necessary if you do find yourself unable to let go of a project or find that the project blocks you from starting something new. But burning the damn thing strikes me as foolish and egotistical, giving the project (and ourselves) more grandeur than we deserve.

If you must get it out of your field of vision to forget about it, put it in a P.O. box and have someone else hold the key. Put it in your mother's attic. Mail it to a friend in a faraway city and ask him or her to hold it for you. Download the files onto a disk and mail it to someone for safekeeping. I say this because an idea that's fundamentally unworkable now may speak to you in two years or five years, revealing itself in new ways. You'll want to be able to go back to the manuscript with your fresh inspiration.

Consider the example of Ha Jin, mentioned in an earlier chapter. He began writing *The Crazed* more than fifteen years before completing it. In the interim he published collections of stories and poems as well as novels. The final version, no doubt, was different from the original idea in profound ways. He was a different person when he finished the book. But he honored his hard work and his material enough to avoid sentimental gestures involving fire.

So put those "bad" ideas in your idea file. You might want to create a "bad" idea file and put in it everything from one-paragraph ideas to complete drafts of novels, memoirs, and scripts. The idea may not be right at the moment, but sometime down the road you may exclaim, "A-ha!" (though I don't know that anyone really says that) and realize how the idea could work. In the meantime, know you've learned much in developing the idea, that the effort has not been wasted, but that the time has come to pursue other ideas that will bear fruit.

 ### Questions to Consider

1. Are you still interested in the idea? Does it continue to reveal itself, if only in elusive bursts of inspiration, or has it become a matter of habit to continue?
2. Is the idea evolving or is it simply becoming a different idea in a succession of different ideas? Have you lost the thread of the initial impulse to develop the idea?
3. What would happen if you abandoned the idea, at least for a while? Can you begin a new project or does the current one still consume you?
4. What are your motives for developing this idea? Are they focused on the idea itself or are they more linked to impressing readers, advancing your career, capitalizing on a trend, landing a contract, unburdening yourself of difficult emotions, making yourself look smart, profound, or worthy of sympathy?

Put It On Paper

PROMPT: Spend the next five writing sessions approaching the troubled idea from new angles, changing the point of view, dramatic context, tone, setting, or some other significant element. After these sessions, read what you've written. Have any of these approaches revealed new ideas about the idea or new energy for developing it? If so, keep going. If not, allow yourself to let go for a while.

PROMPT: Write a few pages about the idea, its meaning and interest for you, your connection to it. Be as honest as you can be as you analyze the connections. Is this idea right for you? Is it clear? Are you bluffing?

PROMPT: If the idea in question is a small one, a new character in a story perhaps, pull the character from the narrative and review how the absence affects the story. Is the character necessary? Is the scene extraneous? Does the stanza call attention to itself or shift the poem into a less appealing direction? If so, let go of the idea. If you're still drawn to it for its own sake, explore it in a page or two of writing. It might be the start of a different project.

PROMPT: Take a week off from developing the idea. After the week, review the idea, reading the pages you've already written. Spend a writing session using the energy the time off has given you. Are new possibilities presenting themselves, or do you find you have little new energy or interest. If the latter is true, it's time to let go.

PROMPT: Develop the idea in a writing session from a different persona. Create a writer who is not you, and make that writer the author of the project in progress. Have fun with this one. Write from a different persona every day for a week, sometimes using the ghost of Jane Austen, other times imagining that a close friend is exploring this idea. This approach can reduce any self-consciousness that might be blocking you. If the idea eludes the likes of Jane Austen or Mark Twain or whomever else you've imagined, perhaps it's not right for you.

Part III

Idea Parts

Chapter Thirteen

Mining for Diamonds

That last chapter was a bit of a downer, I know. But it can feel liberating, too, when you let go of a troubled project or of an idea you've been trying to wedge into a piece. Being able to let go can be a sign that the idea wasn't significant enough for you to pursue anyway. Playwright Marsha Norman (*Night, Mother*) made this point in an interview

> When I have ideas for plays I try to dismiss them immediately so that I only end up writing the plays I *have* to write.

Other writers have made this point in various ways. The cynical part of me questions how "immediately" a writer will dismiss an idea for a project. Let's face it, our love for playing with ideas is why we want to write. Still, Norman's point has value. In fact, it invokes the ultimate test of an idea: Can we live without it? It moves beyond questions of whether an idea is "good" or "bad" and simply lets us know that if we can let go of a project, we probably should let it go. If it continues to interest us, nag us, speak to us while we're driving to work, we may want to give it another try. In this chapter we'll focus on how to do that. How do we find the good stuff in a stalled or troubled piece that, despite its problems, remains important to us?

As we discussed in the first section, resistance to a work in progress isn't always cause for alarm. It's a sign the piece is beginning to assert itself. It's part of the process. But when a piece begins to assert itself like a concert of angry gorillas, you're going to feel . . . a bit concerned. If things get completely out of control, or simply grind to a halt, it's time to focus on what's working and build from there.

Read what you've written so far, and mark the parts that you like, anything from a single word to an entire scene or stanza. Don't question why you like it or try to categorize it, just note it. A dot of your pen in the margin is all that's necessary. When you've finished reading the draft, put it away for a day or two. Let it simmer in your mind. Then ask yourself, every now and again, what comes to mind when you think of the piece. With luck, it won't be the skull-scalding rage at the piece's failings. Instead, one of those images you noted will come to mind. Or the way a character snaps out a line of dialogue.

When you come back to the piece, begin with the image or event or whatever you first think of. Think about what makes that idea so prominent. Does it embody in some way the piece as a whole? What qualities make it unique, resonant, and memorable? Are these qualities apparent throughout the piece? If not, think of ways to expand them. If the element you've chosen doesn't seem to be emblematic of the piece as a whole, explore its relationship to the piece. Does it belong there? Also consider possible connections that you may be missing. Perhaps it *is* emblematic, but you haven't yet realized the connection. You may not yet understand the piece well enough, and this image or detail or whatever is sending signals to you. Even if you don't believe there's a connection, imagine the possibility. If this image were central to the piece, how would the piece change? Focus a writing session or two on exploring possible connections.

Connect the Dots

As you review your draft, note where you've placed a dot in the margin to signify an element that is working well. You may even want to list them on a separate sheet of paper. Look for patterns that emerge as you study these elements separate from the larger piece. It's easier to see the connections between the elements when you separate them from the larger piece. It's also easier to see how much of the troubled draft is going well. Some writers tend to "catastrophize," unable to see that a troubled draft contains much that is good. This exercise will help you see those elements more clearly.

After you can see them, compare them to the piece as a whole. Why are these elements working and why is the overall piece not working, or at least not working as well as you'd hoped? How do the working elements compare in terms of tone, focus, theme, and story to those that are less successful. For example, do your favorite parts tend to involve one character or one place or situation? Do the "good parts" focus on the main idea of the piece or on subordinate ideas. If the latter, consider changing the emphasis of the piece, foregrounding what you had thought was less important but now seems to be the stronger element. If the "good parts" do tend to derive from the piece's primary ideas and goals, what makes you feel the piece is not working? Are there too many elements that distract from the main idea? If so, can some of them be cut or condensed?

Can the ideas or approaches that are working best be expanded? For example, if your essay is a humorous look at today's workplace but seems to be strongest when evoking the sad state of employee morale, perhaps the humor simply was a way in to the subject, a way for you to approach a subject about which you had stronger feelings than you wanted to face. Now that you have a draft in progress, perhaps the humor needs to be shed or at least become a minor, complementary tone rather than the primary thrust of the piece. It can be used as a counterweight rather than dominating the piece. Maybe the piece is feeling constricted because you're not allowing yourself to face less comfortable feelings. You're trying to avoid allowing the piece to become a raging polemic, but in doing so you're hiding behind the humor.

Or perhaps you're writing a screenplay but your efforts to keep the plot moving swiftly along have left your characters undeveloped. And yet, your favorite parts are the moments when the characters reveal themselves in some way. Your list of elements that work mostly contains items pertaining to these moments. If so, you might be forcing the story in directions it doesn't want to go, which is why it feels flat and empty to you, despite a dynamic plot. Expand the moments you like best. Look for ways to explore the characters more deeply without significantly slowing the plot. Consider that the story you want to tell may not need such a fast-moving plot. Are you being too heavily influenced by what you perceive as the expectations of movie producers?

I could offer a dozen more examples, but you get the point. Focus on what's working and use those elements as guides for revising, even reconceiving, the entire piece. When you strip away the elements holding back the piece, you may end up moving forward with something vastly different from the draft you have now. Allow that to happen. Some pieces have slower evolutions than others and require more time to reveal their true natures.

Starting Over

Sometimes you'll find that by isolating the good ideas, you're not left with much. Ten pages of prose might contain only an image or two that you really like. Before abandoning the piece, run through the strategies we've explored in recent chapters: Put it away for a while; listen to the piece and allow it to go its own way; give it to a trusted reader for comment; examine the expectations you have for the piece, the various personal issues that inform our work; try to be objective about the piece and about your expectations, trying to see it clearly. If you're still convinced that the premise is good but your execution poor, consider starting over, this time focusing on the elements that are working in the current draft.

For example, you believe your idea for a short story is a good one and the first few pages work well. Then the piece loses its energy and its focus, it drifts off into dullness and confusion. Okay. Cut everything after those first few pages, and start from there. But before moving ahead and possibly frustrating yourself or feeling blocked, read those first pages several times. Why are they working and how are they working? What do you like about them that's missing in the rest of the draft? Try to get back to that initial burst of inspiration. What was it about that burst that started the piece so well? What goals were you foreseeing? What strengths did you hope the piece would possess? In short, take the one-step-back-two-steps-forward approach. For whatever reason, the piece has lost some of its juice. Try to recover that juice by returning to a place—in your mind as well as on the page—where you still had it.

Perhaps that process is more difficult than simply stripping away pages four through ten and returning to three. Perhaps, as mentioned, you're left with only a few scattered images, an opening situation, a brief exchange in dialogue. That's okay. If you still believe in the generative idea, we have these few elements to build upon. Isolate each of them and brainstorm, taking them together or separately, one at a time. Use them as the core around which to build a new piece, one more reflective of the strengths of those elements.

Apply the method we've discussed throughout the book: Add new ideas to ones already on the page; stay creative and open as you continue to develop the draft; listen to the piece and look for patterns that hold the key to a deep understanding of the piece. As you continue to build around the core ideas, I think you'll find that some of the images, sentences, descriptions, and bits of drama that you cut will make their way back. Not all of them, of course, but more than you planned to salvage. Seen within the context of a reenvisioned draft, they will take on a fresh appeal. You'll also have a richer understanding of the piece itself, gained from the hours of work and struggle you put into the earlier draft. At the risk of sounding like Pollyanna, the time spent on the "failed" draft was not wasted. You'll reap the rewards of those efforts in the next drafts, even ones that are far different from the first.

As you move forward with the salvaged draft, you'll find the piece takes on new energy. More ideas will occur to you and flow into the piece. It's not likely that you'll ride the mad rush that produced the first pages of the piece, but Hemingway talked about the advantages of turning down the burner to a low, steady flame. Within that approach, you'll work more productively. You'll live more completely in the world of the piece, rather than roaring ahead outside of it. Overheard lines will find their way in. Images will appear in your mind as you drive. Characters will speak while you're in the shower. The story will take on a life of its own.

Questions to Consider

1. If the piece isn't working, what elements can you simply not cut? Which ones form the heart of the piece?
2. Are you able and willing to let go of the draft in progress, to salvage what's working and begin again? If so, do you feel a renewed sense of interest? If not, why are you hanging on? Is it the daunting task of beginning again? How might you get past that feeling?
3. Have you taken time to listen to the piece, to allow it to strike its own course? Have you read it aloud to yourself?
4. Is the piece *really* not working or are your expectations for it unrealistic? Are you failing to achieve your goals for the piece, and if so, do those goals need to be evaluated and revised?

Put It On Paper

PROMPT: Before abandoning the draft, read it again and choose three elements—images or descriptions or parts of scenes—that you like, even if they don't fit the rest of the draft. Just liking them is enough. Spend a writing session on each one, brainstorming ideas to develop these elements. Write one or two pages focused on each of the three elements, based on the ideas you created while brainstorming.

PROMPT: Let's build on the previous prompt. In your next sessions, try to pull the previous brainstorms into a somewhat unified piece, fashioning transitions and making connections. Feel free to add new ideas to the piece to harmonize the elements.

PROMPT: Reduce the piece to its frame, its skeleton. If necessary, outline it. Examine how the pieces work together. Isolate those elements that don't fit and brainstorm ways of making them fit. If they still don't fit, outline the piece again without those elements and see if the piece still works.

PROMPT: Using the outline from the previous prompt, look for redundancies. Are two characters doing the work of one? Can the characters be fused somehow or can one character be eliminated? Are two image motifs producing the same effect? Eliminate one and decide if the piece works better that way.

PROMPT: Write a "bizarre" version of the piece, using the same basic elements—setting, characters, plot—but allow yourself to achieve completely different results. Can a melancholy character, for example, perform the same actions but in a comic way? Can a moody atmosphere be made frightening or energetic?

PROMPT: Is there a flaw in the premise of your piece? Look closely at the core idea and decide if it still works for you. If you feel confident in it, brainstorm new possibilities for it, new ideas and new directions.

PROMPT: *Don't* write anything on the piece for at least a week. Do new ideas for it continue to pop into your mind? If so, you've put the project to the ultimate test. If the ideas keep coming or if you're simply nagged by an urge to keep searching for ideas, write about your quest. Try to focus on the source of your desire to move forward with the piece. Elaborate on your interest in it, your goals for wanting to complete it.

Chapter Fourteen

Fish or Foul?

As you move forward in developing and assessing your ideas, consider which form you want to use. For example, though you usually may focus your creative efforts on writing short stories, an idea you're developing might be better suited for a memoir, such as when you're dealing with autobiographical material that doesn't seem to retain its power when developing as fiction. Of course, another idea might require the opposite approach: You're used to writing personal essays, but for some reason a certain episode requires the distance you gain by writing it as fiction.

Choosing the right form for an idea can turn a good idea into a great piece. It can inspire you to be more creative. Choosing the right form can mean the difference between a successful piece and an unsuccessful one. Choosing the right form also can unblock a stalled project. Rather than shelve the project or reject the idea as unworkable, try shifting to a different form and see if that doesn't get your fingers and your imagination moving again.

Sometimes finding the right form is as much a matter of mindset as it is of the particular techniques available in a particular form. We might feel more secure, for example, writing a real-life experience as fiction, even though the fictive story relies mostly on what really happened. The writer Pam Houston made this point at a conference where I heard her speak several years ago. Houston is known for her wonderful short stories, which she has stated a number of times are autobiographical. Several years ago she published a collection of personal essays titled

A Little More About Me. Even the title suggests her awareness of her autobiographical approach in her fiction. At the conference, someone asked her the difference between her stories and essays. She said her stories tend to be 90 percent true and 10 percent fiction. She said her essays also were 90 percent true and 10 percent fiction. Though she clearly had her tongue in her cheek, it was also clear that there wasn't a significant difference between her essays and her stories. The essay form required that she not make up dialogue or fictive transitional events, as she could do in fiction, but it also freed her to stick to reality instead of seeking ways to fictionalize events and situations in her life.

Houston also is a good example in that she works best in the short form—short story and essay. After the success of her first book, a collection of stories titled *Cowboys Are My Weakness*, she began work on a novel. In the publishing world, story collections don't sell nearly as well as novels, so a successful fiction writer is pushed to work in the longer form. Houston tried for several years to finish the novel, which then became the long-awaited novel. We're still waiting. After struggling with the novel, she finally broke it into interconnected short stories and was able to bring together a second collection that enjoyed much success. She still has not published a novel.

Her experience illustrates that sometimes the form we choose can foster creativity or block it. Form can bind us, blind us, or set us free. The novel form wasn't right for Houston, and her attempts to work in that form led to long bouts of writer's block. Of course, she also was coping with the expectations of a large audience still a-swoon over her first book and eager for more, but as soon as she broke the novel into smaller pieces and began writing the book as a collection of linked stories, she no longer felt blocked by those expectations.

Exploring Forms

There's a cliché about writing that says we don't find our stories, they find us. Much the same can be said about form. Let's examine this point in two ways. First, writers sometimes struggle with their projects because they haven't yet found the form in which they work best, the one that allows them to be at their most creative. Not that we have to limit ourselves to one, but sometimes our imaginations and natural abilities blend more easily with a particular form. Stephen King made this point when asked why such a talented and educated writer would work in the horror genre, which often is snobbishly viewed as a sensationalistic, commercial form. He answered by saying something along the lines of "What makes you think I could write any other way?"

Thriller writer David Morrell echoes this belief. Morrell taught at the University of Iowa for many years as a professor of American Literature. His colleagues wondered how a man of his education and accomplishment could be satisfied by writing thrillers. Morrell, like King, explains in his book *Lessons from a Lifetime of Writing* that his imagination responds more passionately to that genre than to literary fiction.

The point is that certain forms will have an intrinsic appeal to us, based on who we are—our interests, beliefs, attitudes, experiences. The qualities of that form are suited to our strengths as writers. If you feel that your inspired beginnings for projects usually end up as false starts, perhaps you're not working in the form that best suits your abilities and proclivities. Perhaps you learned to write in fiction workshops, so you've never tried to write poetry or personal essays. You've simply never explored other options. If that's the case, I recommend spending a few writing sessions on projects in forms other than the one you usually choose. Try poetry. Try memoir. Try a play. The changes in form may spark new ideas or give you new ways to see old ideas. If you're chronically suffering from writer's block or you often feel that you're not achieving your creative potential, perhaps you haven't found your best form or maybe you've too narrowly defined the forms you can explore.

Some writers know which forms best suit them but choose to write in other forms. A writer might be a natural poet but feels there's no commercial market for poetry, so she tries to write novels. Or, a writer might tend to create ideas for quiet, atmospheric stories but may focus his creative efforts on brassier, more action-oriented fiction in hopes of gaining a large audience. Or, in college workshops people tend to write literary fiction, and so a writer might follow suit and pursue this form, despite a natural gift for writing hard-boiled mysteries. The old saw about writing about what you love also applies to writing in the forms that you love. If you want to explore new forms for reasons of commercial success, choose ones that fit your talents.

Making this choice requires understanding your interests and talents. Finding your form requires knowing yourself as a writer. Knowing yourself requires time on the page. The more you write, the better you'll understand your gifts, and you'll be able to make wiser choices about which form to use. Finally, our urge to choose a particular form often involves our goals and our material. Some material is better suited for one form. In an interview with Ann Charters, Grace Paley, an extraordinary poet and fiction writer, explains how she makes decisions about form

> I can give you a definition that can be proven wrong in many ways, but for me it was that in writing poetry I wanted to talk to the world, I wanted to address the world, so to speak. But writing stories, I wanted the world to explain itself to me, so to speak. . . . I had to reach out to it, a very different thing than writing poems.

As Paley developed as a poet, she felt the need for new approaches to her material. She also found that her subject matter was changing, that new material was appearing in her life and her imagination, and she couldn't handle that material in poetry. In the interview, she notes that her need to shift to fiction was a personal one, that another poet might have handled the new material in poetry, but she could not.

That decision takes courage. I regret not making such a decision while writing a short story a number of years ago. As I wrote the story, it grew more apparent to me that the dialogue had a certain theatrical quality, a largeness that didn't fit the narrative texture of the story. At some point I realized that the dialogue was pushing me toward a play, a form I'd never tried before. Rather than pushing in that direction I tamped down the dialogue. The story was published, though the magazine's editor made suggestions for quieting the dialogue even further. I followed these suggestions, but in the years since I've thought the braver choice would have been to break the story open and try it as a play.

Form and Ideas

Being aware of the options available to you in form can help you be more creative and more productive, as well as more successful in your writing. At the same time, some ideas will work best within a particular form, and finding that form can mean the difference between success and failure with the project. If we choose a form that's not right for the idea, the project will collapse at some point, and we'll grumble that the idea wasn't good. The problem, however, was more one of form than idea.

In workshops, I'm often asked "How can you tell what form to use?" This question usually refers to handling autobiographical material, and the writer is unsure whether to fictionalize or to use a nonfiction form. Sometimes the question arises over issues of length—short story or novel, essay or book-length memoir. Sometimes it's a matter of audience—young adult novel or adult novel? And sometimes it's just plain confusing, along the lines of: "I'm working on this story, and it involves solving a murder, but it's not a mystery novel, and there's a prominent love interest, but it's not a romance novel or what some people call women's fiction. It's really kind of a literary piece, a character study. And the story is closely based on an actual murder, but I don't know if I should write the story as a true-crime book. I'm even thinking maybe it should be a screenplay because it would make one hell of a movie. Which form should I choose?"

Uh . . . well. . . .

Unfortunately, there's no formula for choosing the best form for an idea. Often, the idea itself will direct you as you write, which is why it's important to keep an open mind as you begin exploring. Try not to settle too quickly on the form. If the idea develops most naturally as nonfiction, follow that lead. If, however, you find yourself trying to silence imaginary voices, directing the piece toward a fiction approach, try instead to listen to those voices. They may be leading you in a new and more appropriate direction.

Like many other aspects of creative writing, finding the best form for an idea mostly is an intuitive process. If you feel torn between two forms, try one for a while and pay attention to how it's working. Then try the other for a few writing sessions. Which one feels more natural? Which one sparks better ideas or more of your interest? Don't think that working for a little while in a second form is wasted time if you decide to return to the first form. You're learning the subject and exploring the idea even as you write in that second form.

The key is knowing that you have options. If a project stalls, one way to get it going again is to change the form. Perhaps you've exhausted what the idea can do within a certain form, and by switching to another you create many more possibilities. Forms bring with them expectations and conventions that can push the idea in new directions. Explore these possibilities, and you could find yourself moving forward again.

Questions to Consider

1. Which forms suit you best as a writer? Which ones do you enjoy most as a reader?
2. How many forms have you tried using as a writer? Do any forms that you've never tried beckon to you? What keeps you from trying them?
3. Have you found the best form for the ideas you're developing at the moment? Have you considered other options?
4. If you're blocked on a piece, have you considered switching forms? What new ideas and directions might spring from trying a different form? Are these possibilities worth considering?

Put It On Paper

P R O M P T : Explore an idea in three writing sessions by using three different forms. For example, you have an idea for a story involving an undertaker. Write a page of that story as fiction. Do some research and write a page of a nonfiction article about undertakers. Write a page about the undertaker story as a play.

P R O M P T : Pull a stalled idea from your files—a draft of a story, some notes for a project that never was started, whatever you've got. Spend at least two writing sessions developing the premise in a form other than the one you used originally or considered using. And choose a form that's different enough to reframe the project in your mind. For example, if you began developing the idea as short story, switching to a novel isn't going to offer you much that's new. Instead, develop it as a poem or as a screenplay.

P R O M P T : Push forward a stalled idea by using an epistolary or diary form. Have your characters communicate for a while by letter or e-mail. Have a character explore the conflict in a journal entry.

P R O M P T : Push forward a stalled idea by writing a few pages as a children's story (unless, of course, it's already a children's story). This form can help you return to the basics of a story, to see it in an elemental way.

P R O M P T : Push forward a stalled idea by using a form of prescriptive nonfiction (how-to, self-help, etc.) Your story about a troubled family could be reframed as a case study of troubled families or could be reset in step-by-step fashion, along the lines of "Five Steps to Healing Your Family."

P R O M P T : Spend a session brainstorming ideas to fit various forms. For example, if you were to write a romance novel, what story would you tell? If you were to write a coming-of-age novel, what story would you pursue? If you were to write a lyric poem, what subject would you explore?

P R O M P T : Spend a session brainstorming possible forms for ideas in your file that you've yet to begin developing. For example, how would you develop a favorite idea as a screenplay? A memoir? A science fiction novel?

P R O M P T : Read the work of a writer who is successful in a variety of forms, such as Grace Paley, Joyce Carol Oates, John Updike or Denis Johnson. Try to reach some conclusions about why they chose to develop certain subject matter in one form or another.

P R O M P T : If your characters refuse to open up and reveal themselves, an interrogation is in order. You're the cop. Shine the desk lamp in their faces and begin firing your questions. Be relentless. (You can apologize afterward.)

P R O M P T : If the previous prompt is too drastic, interview your characters for a news article or as part of a talk show on radio or TV. You may even want to do this one orally, recording the questions and answers. The format will seem artificial, even a little hokey, I know. But your consciousness of the change in approach and form will make you less focused on the characters and can unlock their stories.

Chapter Fifteen

People

Everything you write involves people in some way, even if only one person and even if that person is you. It's a good idea, therefore, to look for ideas by looking at the people around you. If you're already developing some ideas but feel that things aren't going as well as you'd hoped, try looking at the people on the page. If you're already developing some ideas but want more ideas for the piece, look to your family. Their desires and goals—their observations and attitudes, along with the way all of those things reflect your own—are your primary source of ideas.

In our stories, our characters engage us much more than any other aspect, even plot. It doesn't much matter what happens if we don't care who it happens to. Even in a poem in which no people appear, we are in the mind of the speaker, seeing the images through his eyes. The images take their meaning in part through the person who is presenting them to us. The pleasure of reading any creative project involves getting into someone else's mind, seeing someone else's world through someone else's point of view.

Over the years I've read and written many interviews with writers. In discussing how their various projects were begun and developed, the majority of these writers mention beginning with a character or characters. In this chapter we'll discuss ways of using characters to get ideas for new projects, to get ideas for projects already underway, and to get stalled projects moving again. I'll use the word *character* to include real people who you might use in a personal essay or memoir, as well as unnamed speakers in poems. This approach is less cumbersome than noting the distinction every time fictional characters or real people are mentioned.

Getting Ideas Through Characters

As mentioned above, many projects begin with an idea about a character. Someone you know, perhaps, or someone you see at the grocery store or in your neighborhood. Sometimes an imaginary character will begin speaking to you. Or you might think of a character who has a certain job or hobby or situation that interests you. You have no conflict as yet, no story, but you have a character who engages your imagination in some way.

The key to finding such characters is opening yourself to possibilities. Be aware of the people around you. As we've discussed, keep a notebook with you and use it to jot down descriptions and bits of overheard conversation. Listen to the voices in your mind that pop up with something to say every now and again. For fiction, don't feel duty bound to the real-life models for your characters. Sometimes we're more creative with people we don't know, those we observe on the street or at the mall. We can project entirely imagined lives, using only their appearance or some aspect of their personalities that we notice. Successful writers observe their worlds and allow their imaginations to be actively engaged with those worlds.

While I was in graduate school, the esteemed novelist, memoirist, and photographer Wright Morris held the visiting writer position for a semester. Well into his seventies by that time, Morris made himself available to students, but usually was not seen much unless he was teaching. He spent most of his time at the house on campus where the visiting writer stayed. Not long after he left, he published a short story, I believe it was in *The New Yorker*, about an eccentric couple who roamed the streets of a small town, dressed in odd clothes, a strange pair indeed. In fact, they were very much like a couple that was seen every day on the streets of the university town. There were a good number of writers in the program, some who had lived in the town for years, but none of us had seen the story potential in that couple. Meanwhile, Morris, who seemed to rarely leave the house, saw their potential and turned them into literary characters. It was a rueful lesson for all of us to keep our eyes and imaginations open to the people around us.

You might take a conscious approach to this task, making lists of people who are potential characters. You might dig into your files and look for characters in previous work, notes to yourself about this or that character who seems worth further exploration. Read newspapers and magazines in search of characters. Again, for fiction you don't have to stick with the real-life models. I'd bet that Morris never spoke to that couple and had few facts about them. He imagined their lives and their situation based on his observations, however fleeting. Sometimes one glimpse or a snatch of conversation is enough to get your imagination moving.

Your imagination will begin adding ideas to the initial ideas about a character when you begin putting words on the page. You might begin with simple descriptions, which can lead to scenes, sometimes disconnected scenes, but ones that will help you begin to develop an understanding of the character. Sooner or later a situation will arise from the scenes, a conflict that can be the basis of a story.

Just as you shouldn't feel the need to be loyal to the real-life model for a fictional character, stay open to a character's need to change and grow. In life, we often get a sense of a person at the first meeting, but as we get to know that person we find our initial impressions are limited, sometimes even wrong. The person reveals new layers we didn't sense were there. The same is true for characters in fiction. You limit the possibilities of your stories when you limit your characters, making final decisions about them before you know them well, before you've spent enough time with them to begin peeling back the layers.

If you're writing nonfiction, you can take a similarly conscious approach in developing ideas from people. What people interest you? Who has a story that you'd like to tell? Is there someone you observe on a regular basis? Who is involved in stories focused on your own experiences? Family? Friends? Lovers? Colleagues? Teachers? People from your distant past? People in your life today? Who connects with your own life? These could be people you know or could be famous people that capture your imagination in some way. Is there a personal connection to any of these people? One of my favorite books is Nicholson Baker's *U and I: A True Story*, a personal reflection on his admiration for John Updike. It's a funny, moving, and fascinating study of Updike that also examines the nature of the writing life. Baker had met Updike briefly before writing *U and I* but didn't know him. The book, which began as an essay for *The Atlantic Monthly*, is much more about Baker's own coming of age as a writer than a biographical piece about Updike.

In my own experience, I've written about Pete Rose, the famous baseball star. Rose lived near me when I was a boy, and though I'd never met him before writing the piece, I felt a personal connection to him. Even real-life folks, famous or not, represent in our imaginations aspects of ourselves. You don't need to know the nature of this connection as you begin to write. Sustained interest in the person, whether an uncle or the Pope, suggests some type of connection and one worth investigating on the page.

We won't get into how to develop characters here. There are plenty of good books on the subject if you're seeking advice on that point of craft. The point here is that getting ideas for your writing can be as simple as looking closely at people, ones in real life, ones that spring from your imagination, and ones that exist somewhere in between. If you're feeling your interest in a project waning, look to the characters and focus on generating fresh ideas from them.

Unblocking With Characters

The same holds true if you're blocked on a project. Perhaps you're confused about which direction to take or you're stuck because the piece feels flat. Take time to explore your characters for a while. Within them you'll find many new ideas that can get your project moving again. As I mentioned above, we sometimes circumscribe our characters so narrowly that they begin to grow flat and dull after a few scenes. We have a clear but limited idea about the character and never push beyond that view. They hit the same emotional note time and again, becoming predictable and boring, even to us. Avoid the temptation to scrap the character and the idea. Instead, push deeper. Spend a writing session or two exploring the character, perhaps by taking the character out of the context of the ongoing piece. Root through the character's attic or push him five or ten years into the past. Describe school and family life. Make a list of all the character's romantic relationships.

Sometimes the problem is we don't like a character enough. We don't care enough about her situation or fate. We may not even realize we feel this way. Instead, our readers say they don't like or care about the character and we find ourselves defending him. But in our hearts, we tend to agree. Take time to develop relationships with your characters. Make sure they are people whose stories you're burning to write. Make sure you understand the character's goal—what he or she wants. And make sure that achieving that goal is paramount in the life of the character.

If necessary, raise the stakes for these imaginary people. Make sure the story focuses on a pivotal moment in the character's life. Consider ways of making the moment of the story even more pivotal.

Author Ken Follett wrote a number of novels featuring crime-solving protagonists. These novels didn't sell, and he now feels embarrassed by them. As he developed as a writer, he began telling stories in which regular people—not professional soldiers or crime investigators—were involved in violent situations.

> I prefer to write about ordinary people. My most successful stories are about people who pass through the greatest crisis in their lives during the book. In *Eye of the Needle*, it was the peak moment in her [the character's] life when she killed that spy. I find that much more exciting.

Follett writes historical thrillers, and so the stakes for his characters usually are life or death and the fate of the free world. Even if you're writing stories of a more personal nature, the stakes should seem just as significant to the character. You have to know your character well to know what he or she wants and needs so desperately.

Another situation that can block a project is losing a character under the weight of the plot or the theme. We want to tell a story that explores a philosophical or political idea, and the thoughts and actions of our characters simply reflect the idea. Or we want to tell a story with an active plot, which requires the characters to think and act in certain ways. So they become mere pawns, moving across the chessboard of the story as they need to move in order to advance the plot. At some point in both these situations, we find that we don't care all that much about the story anymore. It all seems contrived and uninteresting.

Once again: Look to your characters. Look for ways to allow the themes as well as the plots to grow more organically from the characters. As you develop your project, be open to how your themes can change. Arthur Miller began his famous play *Death of a Salesman* as a polemic against big business, showing how the common working man is used and then discarded. But as he wrote, Willy Loman (even the name is overly symbolic and vehicular) developed more deeply as a character. His moral confusion, his grasping ambitions, his love for his sons, became much more real than Miller foresaw when he began the project. In fact, the political message now seems dated and narrow, but the story of the Loman family still resonates in powerful ways. If Miller had kept to his initial plans, the play would be an anachronistic political piece, along the lines of "Waiting for Lefty" by Clifford Odets, a far less important and resonant play.

From the same era, consider the film *On the Waterfront*. It was created as a defense by Elia Kazan and Budd Schulberg, who snitched on Hollywood colleagues during the McCarthy hearings. It also exposes the corruption on the docks of New York. Fifty years later, these aspects of the film are little more than interesting background anecdotes. Instead, we remember the famous "I could have been a contender" speech, which addresses a far deeper and more universal truth. We remember the story of ex-boxer Terry Malloy and his struggle against his conscience, weighing moral issues that confront everyone. Through Malloy and the other characters, the film takes on a texture and power far beyond its intended themes.

Think about these examples, or others that you know, when your project has stalled. Also consider the possibility that the early decisions you've made about the plot or structure of your piece are forcing the characters to act in ways that, as the characters develop on the page, no longer seem natural. For example, you're writing a piece about an elderly woman lost in a bustling city on a rainy afternoon, and you're trying to evoke her fears and fragility, knowing that at the climax you're going to have her witness a violent crime. As the story, unfolds, however, it's becoming a quieter piece about the character's recollections of the city as it was fifty years ago, when as a teenager she came here to shop with her friends and to see the latest shows. Perhaps you've decided too quickly that your character is weak and confused, a victim of the cold urban jungle. Rather than feeling blocked on the story, allow the character to lead you to a new story with new goals.

Perhaps you're writing a personal essay about motherhood and have decided to explore your own tempestuous relationship with your mother. You could feel blocked if Mom on the page insists on being a more sympathetic character, the piece allowing you a new understanding of her problems. Yes, your early plans will be tough to execute, but instead of feeling blocked, allow the person on the page to take you in an unforeseen direction.

Allowing characters their latitude is difficult in genre fiction, where plot is king. If your protagonist needs to investigate a murder, well, there had better be a murder and there had better be red herrings and a villain and so on. If you're writing a romance, your leads had better be smitten with each other. If they decide that their love isn't worth the trouble of overcoming the obstacles impeding it, you're not going to be able to complete your romance novel. In genre fiction, the plot directs. Your task, therefore, is to allow the plot to move along while continuing to give your characters enough layers to make them interesting. That's not an easy task, and it's even more difficult for writers with a series character, for whom each case is not a matter of life or death.

Questions to Consider

1. Why are you writing about these characters? Are their stories important to you? How deeply are you invested in telling their stories?

2. Have you allowed your characters to evolve as you develop their stories? Have you kept your mind open to new possibilities with your characters?

3. As your characters continue to reveal themselves to you, do they spark new ideas for the project, new directions and new possibilities?

4. Are considerations such as plot and theme confining your characters? If so, how can you give them a greater sense of depth and freedom? What effect will this have on the project?

Put It On Paper

P R O M P T : Write a page about someone you know, someone who interests you, by presenting them doing something emblematic of their nature. For example, if your character is a caring, selfless person, show them in a situation in which they're demonstrating that trait.

P R O M P T : Picking up on the previous prompt, if you're feeling a character is not as engaging on the page as he or she is in your imagination or memory, review the writing and look for places where the character is demonstrating the traits that most engage you. If you don't find them, create them and move them into the piece.

P R O M P T : Reverse the approach of the first prompt by showing a character doing something that is *not* emblematic of their nature. Have your habitually honest character tell a lie, for example, or have her swipe something from the grocery store.

PROMPT: Are you testing your character well enough in your troubled project? Sometimes we can have a potentially interesting character but simply aren't revealing enough of them because they aren't in any type of conflict. If you're writing fiction, push the conflict for your character. If you're writing nonfiction, consider other situations in which you can present your character, ones that reveal the character at greater depths due to greater pressures.

PROMPT: Write a page or two in which your character performs a task, something at which he excels. Then write a page or two in which the character performs a task poorly. As you write, describe the action so that his abilities, or lack of them, suggest who he is. For example, your character's failure at building a new deck could demonstrate his lack of patience. Your character's success at coaching his son's soccer team could show his ability to understand children.

PROMPT: Write an extended dialogue between two of your characters. Have them discuss a subject that does not appear in the ongoing project. If you don't have an active project, have two characters discuss any subject, though preferably one about which they disagree.

PROMPT: Change one aspect of your protagonist in an ongoing project. Make her taller, for example. Give him a thatch of red hair. If you're writing nonfiction, emphasize some new aspect of your focal person. If you're writing about your uncle's alcoholic ways, for example, also foreground his obsession with the Kennedy assassination.

Chapter Sixteen

You Gotta Have Arc

When we say a story has arc we mean that it has a recognizable structure, some type of rising and falling action. Often it builds to a peak, commonly called the climax, in which the suspense that has been building throughout the story is released. To say a story has arc doesn't mean necessarily that it has a traditional beginning-middle-end structure. It doesn't mean that events are ordered chronologically. It does mean you've ordered the events into some type of shape no matter what genre you've chosen. In this chapter we're going to talk about shape. Whether you use the term "plot" or "structure" or some other term doesn't matter. We're focusing on how to get ideas for creating and sustaining suspense, positing a conflict of some sort that the reader wants you to resolve in a satisfying way. The range of what we mean by suspense is very wide. In a thriller, the survival of the world might be at risk. In a quiet, literary story, a character may be deciding about something inconsequential to anyone else.

The question of shape gives rise to many other questions of storytelling. The other day my son, who has been fiddling with a fantasy-adventure story, asked me "How do you know where to start?" He's only thirteen, but the question is one that has confounded writers for hundreds of years. Other questions involving shape are: How do you know where to end? How do you supply enough information to keep the reader interested without giving away the ending? How do you supply the important background information without stopping your story and losing your reader?

After those questions come the questions of how best to order the events. Chronologically? Cause and effect? Then we face the question of which events to dramatize and which ones to present in narrative. How best to create and sustain tension? How to keep the reader gratified while simultaneously delaying gratification until the end? And so on.

If you're asking these questions, you're on the right track. To answer them we must generate ideas. When you're beginning a new piece it's often best not to worry so much about structure. You're still playing with the basic notions. Take time to explore them. An easy way to block yourself early in the process is to begin concocting a structure before you've had time to find out what you're writing.

For example, you have an idea for a character who is based on someone you see regularly at a nearby convenience store. He's a shaggy-haired guy who mumbles a lot to himself. Sometimes he strikes you as insane, other times merely eccentric. Take time to brainstorm some ideas with that character as your focus. Describe him on paper. Consider changing some fundamental aspect about him if you're writing fiction. Explore possibilities for what he might do—ride the bus for hours though he has no place to go, play the lottery fanatically, eat a box of Milk Duds every day. One of the scenarios will spark and you can follow where it takes you. At that point, you might think about structure. Until then, it's not time yet.

As your piece develops, you'll add more ideas to the initial one, as we've discussed earlier in the book. These ideas will dictate your structure, to some extent. They'll develop out of the fundamental question: What happens next? To answer that question well, we need to keep creating new ideas. We need to develop the narrative line in a way that seems natural to the reader but not obvious, predictable, or mundane. Once again, in writing stories so much is a matter of balance. It's impossible to generalize about how to achieve this balance, but I'll risk an assertion: In the early stages of working on a piece, don't worry a lot about creating logic and continuity. If you've been calling the character "Devlin" for two weeks and suddenly his name is "Fisher," let it go. Make the change. Surprise yourself in what the character might do, how the plot might twist. In the later stages of the process, you still need to be creating ideas, but you've established the rules of the piece and need to adhere to them. If you've established that your character is terrified of conflict, you can't have that character launch into a diatribe at his boss, unless you've shown the character moving toward that end or shown the character breaking down in some way.

If you're writing popular fiction, the plot is paramount. You need to focus on twists and surprises more than on character and atmosphere. The best writers in these genres manage to develop strong characters with internal issues even as the plot keeps turning corners, but creating a fast-moving plot is the main order of business. For an apprentice writer in any form, it's not a bad idea to read some plot-driven work. The mechanics of the plot are quite clear in this type of work, and it's easy to see, if you're reading as a writer, how the piece is constructed.

Another effective way to learn about structure is to read work by good writers a number of times. On first reading, we can't understand how a piece is structured because we don't yet know what happens in the end. But when we know the story we can go back and read it again and notice how certain events are foreshadowed, how the writer unified the piece, how the writer led the reader to the conclusion.

One Goal at a Time

No matter what type of narrative you're writing, you'll write it one sentence at a time, one scene at a time. To keep the ideas flowing, try thinking in terms of goals—your goals, the reader's goals, the characters' goals. When you begin writing, you may not be sure of the larger goal yet. You have only a character or a situation or a topic. As you write, you'll begin to sense your purpose or at least be at a place where you can ask yourself about your goal in writing the piece. Is it to entertain the reader? To inform the reader? To explore a concept or a character? To resolve a conflict for your character or for yourself? You also need to know the reader's goal in reading the piece. What need or desire in the reader will your piece gratify? Finally, what does the principal character want? If it's nonfiction, the main character may be you or a persona you assume on the page. For example, in his classic essay "Frank Sinatra Has a Cold," Gay Talese is trying to interview Sinatra in order to help fans of the singer understand him better, to provide a behind-the-scenes look at a celebrity. If you're writing an essay on, say, friendship, your goal is to investigate that topic in an interesting way, and the reader follows your quest through your voice.

If you have an instinctive sense of these larger goals, you may not have to ask yourself directly, but you do need to know. With that main goal in mind—for you, the reader, and the character—you begin building the piece, developing it through setting and achieving (or thwarting) smaller, more immediate goals that will lead to the larger one. Therefore, to get ideas for the piece, focus on those goals, taking them one at a time. At its most basic level, that means asking yourself: What does my character want in this scene? What is her goal? How does achieving that goal lead to achieving the larger goal? Again, popular fiction can be a good guide to understanding structure because the goals—immediate ones and the larger goal—are easy to discern. The investigator's goal is to solve the case. In each scene he seeks information—an immediate goal—that leads him to that larger goal. In literary fiction or nonfiction, the goals are presented with more subtlety, but you can discern them if you read the work several times.

By focusing on immediate goals that grow naturally out of the stated or implied conflict and lead to the larger goals of the piece, you can guide yourself from beginning to end. Of course, this process isn't always easy. Sometimes we're not sure about a character's immediate goal. Or we know the immediate goal but struggle with how best to present it.

Another way to get ideas through structure is to decide early that you're going to take a particular structural approach. You're going to tell the story through several characters, each of them offering a subplot that will link to—or from—the main one. Or you're going to use a series of flashbacks. Or you're going to use a mosaic approach, piecing together the story through smaller, seemingly unrelated stories. Michael Cunningham uses this approach brilliantly in his award-winning novel *The Hours*. Or you're going to play with the time sequence, moving forward and back rather than working chronologically. Quentin Tarantino's film *Pulp Fiction* is a fine example of this approach, surprising the audience by including a character in the final scene who we watched die in a previous one.

An experimental approach demands a degree of technical mastery, but it's fun to try them, and they can spark fresh ideas. You may want to play with such alternatives for a while, building some ideas, then move to a more traditional structure with your fresh material in hand. Or if the experimental approach seems to be working, continue to develop it. Moving beyond the tried-and-true will develop your skills and make you more aware of your options for telling a story. Moving beyond literary terrain that feels safe also puts you in a mindset for discovering many new ideas.

When You're Stuck

At the most basic level, writers find themselves stuck at the level of plot more than on any other element of storytelling. By that I mean, when we're stuck on a story, it's usually because we don't know what happens next. We've developed an idea to a certain point and then hit a wall. We explore a few ideas, moving the story in this direction, then that direction, but no direction seems like the right one to take.

Often we hit that wall because we've reached the end of a narrative thread and don't know how to tie onto the next thread. In a famous example, Mark Twain used the Mississippi River to give structure to his novel *The Adventures of Huckleberry Finn*. Jim and Huck move down the river on a raft, and the shape of the river gives shape to the novel. When they miss the confluence of the Ohio River, which would lead them north and to Jim's freedom from slavery, the novel takes a major turn. Twain uses an episodic approach in this novel, allowing his characters to move from the raft onto land to have an adventure before returning them again to the larger goal of the story—freedom. The river supplies the narrative thread that unites these episodes into a cohesive whole. But when Jim is captured and the story moves firmly away from the river, Twain faced that daunting question we all face as writers: What happens next? He stalled on the novel for more than two years. Without the river to guide him, he had no clear sense of direction. He still had the larger goal in mind—freedom for Jim and for Huck—but the narrative thread of the river that had given him a reliable touchstone to which he had been able to return, was gone. His characters had left the river. As we all know, he hauled old favorite Tom Sawyer into the story and managed to finish the novel, though many readers have difficulty with the book from that point on. When Sawyer arrives, the tone of the story changes, taking on elements of broad farce that undermine the complexity of what came before. The characters of Huck and Jim had been deepened by the journey, and the shift to making them comic figures just didn't work. The final section smacks more of Twain's trademark "shtick" than a serious novel. He fell back upon what he knew his audience at the time would recognize and accept.

Critics may be right about this flaw, but as writers we are less quick to denounce him, having struggled with such blocks ourselves. If you're blocked on a piece, ask yourself if you've reached the end of a thread. Have you abandoned whatever you'd been using as a connective device? Is it possible to find a new one?

Another way to use structure to unblock a piece or to ignite renewed interest in it is to allow yourself to veer off course, if only for a short time. By off course, I don't mean to lose sight of the larger goals of the piece. But perhaps it's time to take a somewhat different approach. If your character has been on a lock-step path to the ultimate goal, throw something new in her path. Allow her to get a little lost. If you're blocked because she already *is* lost, then of course you need to redirect and get her back on course.

Another possibility is to push deeper into the structural elements that have been working throughout the piece. For example, if I may presume, Twain might have considered that the river is a significant structural device in his novel. In fact, it had become a character in its own right. By pushing his main characters off the river, he lost a significant element of the story. He could have tried finding a way to put them back on the river and allow them to float, literally and figuratively, to a more natural conclusion. This may or may not have worked. He may have tried that approach without success. I don't know. But I offer it as an illustration of how you can look at an important unifying element in the structure of your piece and decide if you're stuck because you've moved away from it.

One final tip: You can block yourself in terms of structure by holding onto the idea that a particular event *has* to happen. I've worked with many writers who made this claim. "I have to have the character go into the bar because that's where he meets the guy who comes in later in the story. It *has* to happen." Sometimes they're right. But there have been many times in which we were able to find alternatives to whatever had to happen, and things started moving again.

 ### Questions to Consider

1. Are you satisfied with the structure of your current piece of writing? If so, what elements do you like? If not, what one move could you make that gives the structure more interest?
2. Do you tend to use similar structures in your pieces? If so, try a slightly different approach sometime soon. Allow yourself to explore new possibilities.
3. Do you usually outline your pieces before writing them? If so, skip the outline next time. If you don't normally use one, try that approach.
4. Do you usually get ideas for pieces by thinking about plot— a series of events—or by developing a character? There's no right or wrong answer, but give the question some thought.

Put It On Paper

PROMPT: Write a first sentence in which you establish some type of conflict. Then expand that conflict, complicating it in some way, in a few more sentences. If you want, you can use the following sentence to get you started: "When [blank] first found out about [the conflict or situation], [he/she] didn't believe it."

PROMPT: Write a sentence in which some situation is resolved. Don't give all the details; just convey some sense of conclusion. If you want, use this one: "[He/she] shuffled slowly away, leaving the wreckage of the moment, and the past, behind [him/her] forever." Then move backward, writing the paragraph that leads up to that moment. If possible, keep going—backward, of course.

PROMPT: Think of a place that you know well—your home, perhaps, or a nearby park. Pick three locations within that place and set a short scene in each or write briefly about each place. If you can, try to connect the three short pieces in some way.

PROMPT: Write briefly about three particular times in your life: your sixteenth birthday, May 1990, and March of last year. When you finish, look for some connections between them. Try to tie them together if only in a loose way.

PROMPT: In his classic film *Rear Window* Alfred Hitchcock peeks into the lives of several tenants in a New York apartment building. Some of their stories intersect. Others don't. Make yourself the landlord of a four-family building and tell us briefly about the people who live in each apartment, using the building itself as a device for bringing together the stories of the tenants.

PROMPT: If you're stuck, read what you've written and find a spot where you've summarized an event rather than dramatized it, perhaps because you felt it wasn't worth dramatizing. You might be right.

Nevertheless, take a little time and explore that event in a scene.

PROMPT: Spend a session exploring a minor character, placing her in the foreground of her own separate story. When you finish, consider ways of creating a subplot to the main story by giving this character greater prominence.

PROMPT: If you've finished a draft of your story, read it with an eye toward flashback. Cut every one that you find. Then read the story again. Do you really need the flashbacks? Put back only the information that's absolutely essential.

PROMPT: As a variation on the previous prompt, cut only the first flashback. I don't know how many stories I've read in workshops and in contests that open with a strong scene, then, following a space break, retreat to a flashback. The writer is thinking that the opening scene will hook the reader, and so a certain amount of information now can—and must—be relayed. It's a predictable structure and more often than not the story immediately loses energy. Force yourself to move from that first scene to another dramatic situation.

PROMPT: Writers and sumo wrestlers both have to fight against sagging middles. Often we'll hone our opening pages to perfection and will spend equal time and effort getting the ending right. The middle of the piece, however, is overlooked. It's seen as a vehicle for moving the reader from the opening section to the closing one. Take time to outline your middle pages, looking for places to tighten or to raise the dramatic stakes.

Dot the Dragon's Eye

Hualong dianjing is a phrase used in Chinese painting and roughly translates to "Dot the dragon's eye, and it comes to life." It refers to the need for including the key detail in a painting. When the painter takes time to dot the center of the dragon's eye with the tip of the brush, the dragon seems to gain the ability to see. It comes alive on the canvas. The admonition also speaks to the need for including the right details. A painter can brocade the dragon's tale with intricate scales of many sizes and hues, but without the dot in the eye, the dragon will remain dead on the canvas.

The applicability of this statement to writing isn't difficult to see. When we take time to present the details, our writing comes to life. If we focus only on big strokes, the writing remains generic, abstract, and lifeless. Henri Troyat makes this point (with a well-chosen detail of his own) when he writes,

No detail must be neglected in art, for a button half-undone may explain a whole side of a person's character. It is absolutely essential to mention that person's button. But it has to be described in terms of the person's inner life, and attention must not be diverted from the important things to focus on accessories and trivia.

In my experience as an editor and teacher, no other aspect of craft leads to unsuccessful stories more than the lack of specific details and

poorly chosen details. Most apprentice writers have seen enough movies—
if they haven't yet read enough books—to have a basic understanding of
structure. Though they fret about whether to use past tense or present
tense, the question of point of view, while important, often doesn't speak
to the core trouble in the project. Most often, the writer hasn't evoked the
world of the piece, its people and the place and the situation. Through the
details we select we guide our readers, showing them what they need to
see. Through the details we present the characters, as in Troyat's "button
half done."

Too often apprentice writers perceive details as merely lending atmosphere to a piece, describing what the walls look like, the scent of a
budding meadow. The details of the place need to do more than create
atmosphere. Each should be chosen for its effect on the piece. It should
be there for a reason.

Moreover, the details should be specific. Most apprentice writers
know this law of narrative. We learn the need to write "tulip" rather
than "flower," "BMW" rather than "car." But the lesson doesn't end
there. The fact that the flower is a tulip directs the reader in some way,
reflects on the character admiring or holding the tulip, brings in the
varied connotations of a tulip in the reader's mind. The tulip evokes the
physical world of the piece and speaks to its inner world. If "tulip" is
an arbitrary choice, it doesn't have much meaning within the context of
the piece and doesn't give the reader anything more than a visual marker.

The lack of specific, telling details creates a sense of emptiness and
confusion. Inexperienced readers complain that *it's boring* or that "I
didn't *get* it." Often a writer will conclude that the premise is dull or that
the ideas aren't good, but that's not necessarily the case. It may be a
matter of finding the key details that will bring the story to life. It may
be a matter of emphasizing certain details and subordinating or cutting
others. It may be a matter of examining the details in an early draft and
looking for patterns that hold the key to the essence of the piece. By
focusing efforts in this area the writer can find a new understanding and
feel a renewed interest. The piece then can move forward.

You probably will find yourself in this situation as you write: You show a story to your writers group and receive wildly different interpretations of it or hear a whole lot of confusion going on. This response shows you that the story isn't yet on the page, but it doesn't mean the ideas are weak. It may be a matter of guiding the reader by selecting and presenting details more effectively. Every writer has suffered through this situation. Often it's a matter of assuming a piece is finished too soon. Time to go back and reinvestigate it, to bring those key details to the fore.

Even if you don't show it to other writers, you might find yourself feeling that the piece lacks a certain wallop. You're satisfied with the structure and feel your characters are working. What's missing? Why is the piece just sort of *okay* but really not riveting or moving in the way you'd intended? Put it away for a little while, then read it with an eye for the details. Is there a way of using a detail to embody a certain theme that you've spoken to directly and thereby lost the juice of it? Is there a detail in the story that you can develop into a motif or pattern, recalling it throughout the piece in an affecting way? Is there a key detail mentioned early in the piece that you might mention again at the end, giving the detail, and the ending, an extra bit of resonance while giving the piece a stronger sense of unity and closure?

Putting In and Taking Out

So how do you know which details bring the dragon to life and which ones just make the dragon's tail longer? Unfortunately, there's no easy answer and no answer that applies to every situation. You must find the answer with every piece you write. However, there are ways to improve your odds of finding it. First, you have to understand your habits and tendencies as a writer. Does your style tend to include many details or few? Do you often write long, lush descriptions that serve mostly to create atmosphere and show off your language skills? Or perhaps your descriptions serve your stories well but simply tend to run long. Do you fear seeming too obvious in using details as signposts and therefore obscure them whenever possible? Do you tend to have an instinctive sense of where to place and repeat certain details?

In a famous exchange of letters, Scott Fitzgerald and Thomas Wolfe debated their approaches to narrative. Though they were discussing issues beyond details, encompassing all the elements of storytelling, their views are appropriate to our discussion in this chapter. Responding to Fitzgerald's claim that highly selective writers were the real geniuses, Wolfe wrote,

> You say that the great writer like Flaubert has consciously left out the stuff that Bill or Joe will come along presently and put in. Well, don't forget, Scott, that a great writer is not only a leaver-outer but also a putter-inner, and that Shakespeare and Cervantes and Dostoevsky were great putter-inners—greater putter-inners, in fact, than taker-outers. . . .

While reading this passage, I'm comforted by the realization that discussions of craft between literary giants feature no more erudition than what I find in similar discussions with my friends, and I hope you are too. "Putter-inners"? Not exactly the type of phrase you'll want to tape to your computer or to drop oh-so-casually into conversations at the next literary fete. Wolfe liked to conceal his erudition behind a big-country-boy persona. He's well aware of what he's talking about. It's interesting to note that Wolfe was very much a *putter-inner*, while Fitzgerald was a *taker-outer*, and so their views reflect their own approaches to writing.

Consider your approach. Are you a taker-outer or a putter-inner? How does this approach help your work, and how does it hinder your work? Are you putting in the right elements—a telling detail or two rather than hunks of exposition and explanation? Are you taking out the right elements—unnecessary and redundant passages and scenes, allowing the reader to make discoveries? As writers we need to know what to put in and what to take out. In fact, that process is the essence of storytelling. Anyone can simply spill the facts of "what happened" onto a page. It takes a writer to organize those facts into a compelling story, to select the most important details and discard others, to emphasize certain elements and subordinate others.

After we have a draft we examine the details that bring the piece to life. We look for patterns of details and ask ourselves how these patterns shape the story. We ask ourselves why, for example, that eucalyptus tree in the front yard keeps inching into every scene? Why do we note three times that the protagonist carries a sharpened crayon in her purse wherever she goes? We note, also, where details are missing: Where characters are standing in relation to each other during a pivotal conversation, the look on a character's face, the length of the metal pipe the character hides under the driver's seat.

These details bring the piece to life and help you guide the reader to certain themes, but they also ensure that your reader is not distracted by questions sparked by the lack of specific details. If the length of the metal pipe is not important, you tell the reader it's not important by not bothering to describe it. On the other hand, if the pipe plays a key role you tell that to your reader by providing a more specific description. If it does play a key role and you *don't* describe it, your reader may wonder about it, leading to questions that disturb the tension you're trying to create in the piece.

Detail Ideas

In your writer's notebook, create a place for jotting down details that occur to you or that you observe as you go about your day. They can spark ideas for a new piece, and they can spark ideas for work that's ongoing. When you're feeling stale or blocked, flip through your notebook and read the details you've collected there—a smashed pumpkin in the middle of a street, the smell of old books unearthed from a box in the attic, the way a friend's mouth crooks whenever she's trying to be clever, the smell of earthworms after a spring rain, and so on. You might find one that's a good fit for the piece in progress. Or a detail might spark a new idea for the piece.

As we discussed, writers need to be observant. If you keep your eyes open, you'll fill your notebook in a month. As you fill your notebook, you'll see that you notice certain types of things more than others. Your cache of details, for example, will include a lot of faces or gestures or cars or natural images. You might be particularly aware of smells or sounds. Or you might notice details that suggest a certain mood. As you review the details in your notebook, you'll learn about yourself as a writer. You may want to review pieces you've written to find out if the tendency you noticed in the notebook carries over to your stories. For example, do your stories rely heavily on one type of sense? Are the details mostly suggestive of a certain mood? Can you vary your pattern a bit, adding sounds and smells, for example, to a piece that's largely visual?

For some reason I write down interesting signs that I see—billboards, in front of churches, on streets and along highways. Recently, a store near my house closed. It had sold jewelry and fabric and statuary from India and was called Divine Miracles. One day while out for a jog I noticed the store was empty, leaving behind only the message: "Divine Miracles—Out of Business." That one went into the notebook.

Questions to Consider

1. How does the effective use of details make your work stronger? How could you focus on details to enliven an on-going piece?
2. What are the key details at work in a piece you've written that you particularly like?
3. How do writers whom you particularly admire use details to make their work rich and compelling?
4. Are you writing down the details you observe in your notebook?

Put It On Paper

PROMPT: If you're stuck on a piece or disappointed with its results, read it with an eye for the details. Make a list of the key details and find ways to amplify them, perhaps by repeating them or by describing them more fully.

PROMPT: Create a specific detail for each of your characters—or for characters you plan to use in a future piece. Freewrite about each character, noting as many details as possible. Choose one or two that evoke the essence of the character. For example, a character who is very neat and well organized (and perhaps a bit controlling) could be evoked by precise descriptions of their clothing—not a thread out of place.

PROMPT: To make a character surprising and complex, add a contradictory detail. Does your neat-as-a-pin, control-freak character from the previous prompt decorate his bedroom with posters of heavy metal bands?

PROMPT: Go on a detail hunt. Take a walk in your neighborhood and jot down all the interesting details you observe. If you feel the neighborhood is too familiar for you, go to a different one. Focus on sensory impressions, and while looking for the extraordinary don't ignore the ordinary.

PROMPT: Go on a detail theft. Read a piece of fiction or nonfiction (or poetry for that matter) and steal a detail you like. Use it to begin a piece of your own or add it to an ongoing piece. Don't feel guilty. Details take on their significance mostly through the context of the piece itself. Therefore, if you steal a cold bucket of chicken from

Raymond Carver or a hunk of rope from Katherine Anne Porter it quickly will become your own.

PROMPT: Review a piece in progress with an eye for seemingly insignificant details—a character's brown hair, a piece of leftover birthday cake, a neighbor's dog. Freewrite about a detail, expanding its role and importance, perhaps making it the center of its own piece. Then decide if it can take a more important role in the piece in progress.

PROMPT: If you're stuck on a piece, try to find which detail "dots the dragon's eye." Which one brings the piece to life—or could bring it to life if it were more prominently or more effectively placed. If you can't find that "dot," ask yourself which detail definitely could not be cut. If you had to keep only one, which would it be?

PROMPT: Freewrite about a place, either one in a piece you're writing or one you may write someday. Load on the details. Then step back and choose three or four of the most telling ones, the ones that evoke the essence of the place. Cut most of the others and subordinate those you do decide to keep while giving prominence to those few details that are most important.

PROMPT: Write a scene in which characters are *not* confronting an issue between them. They're discussing something else. For example, a married couple has a running feud about moving to a new city. She wants to go; he wants to stay. But rather than argue about it, they talk about plans for this year's garden. Use a detail to suggest the undercurrent. For our couple's scene, you could use a gardening catalogue that has arrived in the mail.

PROMPT: Read a piece you've written and cut five details from it, ones you feel aren't essential to the piece. Then add five details to it. How has it changed? To extend the exercise, choose two details that are mentioned only once or twice and find ways to mention them at least two more times. How has their meaning changed within the piece?

Chapter Eighteen

The Relativity of Truth

S orry for the philosophical chapter title. We're really not going to get into such heady arguments here. We're going to discuss point of view, particularly as it relates to generating ideas for your writing and even more particularly as it relates to getting the most from the project at hand. Point of view, as you know, is one of the most important elements of storytelling. It's not merely a strategy for telling the story, in many ways it *is* the story. One person's tale of lost love is another person's story of escape from a bad relationship. An account of your winning an award in high school will change when told from your perspective as a teen, your perspective today, the perspective of your mother or father, the perspective of the runner-up. Each perspective covers the same actions, the same basic facts, but each is different. A detective's story of hunting for a criminal involves looking at clues and putting together the facts, interviewing bystanders and witnesses. The same story told from the criminal's viewpoint is one of being hunted, of trying to cover up clues, of grappling with doubt and guilt and fear.

If you want further proof, invite some old friends to your place for an evening's trip down memory lane. Bring up experiences you shared—the big prom night that got out of control or the trip to Mexico. You'll find that everyone has different memories of the event or different opinions about it. You might remember an event as a joyous celebration while someone else recalls it with a pang of melancholy or remorse. Each retelling of the events will have different emphasis, different meaning, different moments of significance.

Thus, even if you're writing a memoir, the "truth" you're relating can be presented in different ways, from different perspectives, thus the relativity of that truth. A common exercise to illustrate this point: Write about a personal experience using first person present tense, then first person recollection, then third person recollection, then third person objective. You'll find that each viewpoint will create its own priorities and tone, and will change what you remember. If you're writing fiction, in which the "facts" can be changed at will, the viewpoint can have an even greater influence on the story.

Point of view, therefore, is more than a matter of pronouns—*he* or *she* or *I* or *they* or *we*. It's more than a matter of verb tense—Bill *sees* Carol walking toward him; Bill *saw* Carol walking toward him. Point of view is the fundamental vision of the piece. It influences what happens and how that happens and how the reader responds to what happens. A case in point: A friend told me not long ago that she was changing the point of view of her novel from third person to first person and that she had finished changing most of the "she's to I's." In my mind, that's not a true change in point of view. It's fine to change the pronouns and observe the results on the page. Sometimes that change will be enough to give the story what it needs. But a true change in point of view requires, even forces, a new vision of the story.

A New Perspective

If a project isn't working or isn't giving you what you want from it, or even if you want to explore alternative approaches to the material, it's a good idea to check the point of view. Play with some possibilities. If you've been chugging along in first person, for example, and find that you need some distance from the material, shifting into third person may do the trick. Conversely, if you have set your piece in third person and find that it lacks the visceral wallop you'd intended, a shift to third person could be the answer. These moves, of course, are the most obvious ones. I can't count how many times I've heard such suggestions in workshops or have heard from writers that someone has given them such advice. Sometimes it's advice worth taking.

But not always. And often it doesn't supply the unfettered freedom we hope to find in it. It's human nature to want a quick fix that will answer all the questions, hurdle all the obstacles. We want the "A-ha" moment that will get our fingers tapping the keyboard again. A shift in point of view can have that effect, can release whatever was blocking our progress or give the story a more natural sound. Understand, however, that the shift in point of view won't necessarily be the key that unlocks all doors.

Be aware that every choice you make brings with it a new set of concerns as well as solutions. The shift from third to first, for example, may provide a sharper sense of immediacy, but now certain passages that held a dispassionate distance, that gave a certain somber irony to the piece, are lost. The first person could limit access to a key scene or two, which requires that the character be *in* the scene or have some believable avenue to the information relayed in the scene. The more immediate first-person voice, while providing energy, also can make us less discerning about what to include and what to leave out. It can entrance us with its rhythms. Suddenly the darn thing seems out of control! Sound familiar? Such is the writer's life.

The key is to play with possibilities in point of view. Try several viewpoints and spend enough time with each one to grow comfortable with it, to be able to weigh its advantages and limitations. Fiddling around with your options is more easily done early in the process, before the piece, and its point of view, take on a feeling of inevitability. Give yourself time to explore various points of view as the piece begins to take shape. Allow the focus to shift from one character's point of view to another. Maybe spend a session or two casting a scene or passage in several points of view. By playing around with viewpoint early in the process, you can make a more informed decision when you're ready to commit to one.

When I've offered this advice in the past, some writers say they feel such exploration is a waste of time. They say something like, "The pages I write in first person won't appear in the final piece. I've spent all that time for nothing." They admit that playing with options lessens the chance that the point of view will break down when the piece is underway, but they insist they usually can tell which viewpoint is right without going through the hassle of using several.

I have to disagree, for the reasons mentioned previously. Exploring a few options can generate material the writer most likely would not have discovered through a single viewpoint. If you tried the earlier exercise, you noticed that new details and observations crept into the recollection when you switched points of view. For example, a writer recalling a childhood experience from her adult perspective may remember the emotional tenor of the experience and can summon insights about it within the context of her life since that time. However, when she switches to a present-tense rendering of the event, setting herself in the mind of the child experiencing the event, she'll remember many more particular details, some she may not have thought about since the event took place. In the child's point of view, she won't be able to understand the event at the depth of an adult, and so this version will have fewer observations of that type. By combining the best material of both versions, the writer will have a richer account of the experience than focusing on what either version would offer. And so has the time it took to write it both ways been wasted?

The same is true in getting to know your characters. If you're willing to take time to explore a character's world through the character's point of view, you'll gain a richer understanding of him or her and valuable insights and details, as well. It's worth taking the time even if the character is not supplying the viewpoint of the piece. Of course, you don't need to do that for a character whose role in the piece is very minor or vehicular—a walk-on who appears to swell the narrative crowd a bit. But if, for example, you're writing a coming-of-age novel from the viewpoint of the coming-of-ager, it could be helpful to dip into the minds of other characters to get to know them better. Though the exercise won't be placed fully into the novel, I'll bet you will pick up some good details and a better understanding of that character. The exercise also might spark new ideas for the characters and the novel.

Breaking Blocks With Point of View

As you can see, point of view can be a good source of ideas. It can lead to a fuller understanding of a piece, the characters and situations. It also can help you revive a dormant or blocked project and can energize a project that's moving along but seems to be losing momentum. As we discussed, don't assume it will be the Magic Key that unlocks all doors. Instead, allow it to be a step toward the place you want to go. The shift in viewpoint certainly can shed light on a story. With that light, you can discern what's holding the story back, where you may have taken a wrong turn.

Sometimes a writer will begin a story using the protagonist as viewpoint character, but as the story unfolds it becomes clear that another character needs to be the center of attention and provide the viewpoint. A shift to that character can bring the project to a new level and can ease the struggle of writing it. If you've given up on a story, placing it in the false-start file and yet still feel it's worth reviving, play with the point of view. Examine how the one you've chosen is working in the story, and ask yourself questions. What advantages is the viewpoint offering you? How is it helping the story? How is it the best, most obvious and necessary one to use? How would the story change if you changed the point of view? Would the changes be more positive than negative? What new challenges would a change present?

Don't be afraid to make radical adjustments. In the blocked story, find the character who engages you most other than the viewpoint character. Spend a session writing from the engaging character's viewpoint. Try this move even if you're writing a memoir from your own first-person viewpoint. If you're feeling stifled or self-conscious about your own voice, the switch may free you to write more easily.

A radical adjustment may require a radical approach. In his short novel *The Barracks Thief*, Tobias Wolff uses a variety of points of view while telling the story through a single character. He begins in a distant third person, presenting backgrounds and details about a number of characters. Then he moves to first-person past tense for several chapters, then shifts to first-person present tense for a short time, then eases back into first-person past tense. Through this approach he is able to manipulate the story and the reader's proximity to it, moving us forward and back depending on his goals in the chapters. It's a risky approach that requires great technical skill. I'm not recommending it, but as writers it's good to know—and to explore—our options.

In the Prompts section we'll look at specific ways for handling different situations with point of view. The main point to remember: Know why you're using the viewpoint you're using. Know how it's working to further your ends in the piece, how it's helping you to accomplish your goals.

Questions to Consider

1. Do you usually use the same point of view in your work, tending to favor first person or third person or whatever? Why? Is it time to try new approaches?
2. In an ongoing piece, are you using the most appropriate and effective point of view? How would the piece change if you switched point of view?
3. Have you ever written from the point of view of a character or real-life person far different from yourself? If not, why not give it a try? If so, what were the challenges involved?
4. Who is your all-time favorite point of view character? Why does he or she work so well for you?

Put It On Paper

PROMPT: If your answer to question number three was no, write a few pages from the point of view of someone much different from you. If your answer was yes, give this one a try anyway. Make sure you choose a character far different from you, as well as far different from the character you'd already used.

PROMPT: Write a page from the point of view of a character of a different race or gender from you.

PROMPT: If you're blocked on a piece because your point-of-view character isn't compelling enough, switch to a different character.

PROMPT: If you're blocked because your character isn't likable enough, switch to the point of view of a character who admires the other character.

PROMPT: If you're blocked because the point of view is too confining, vary the viewpoint, switching among several characters. Be sure to make the shifts easy for the reader to assimilate. In other words, don't jump willy-nilly.

PROMPT: If you're blocked because the point of view limits your access to key scenes, especially if you're in first person, shift to third person and allow yourself to use several viewpoints.

PROMPT: If you usually write in first person, stop. Especially if your first-person characters are similar to you. Shift to another character. First person would seem to be the easiest approach, but using it well is difficult and requires a certain level of experience.

PROMPT: Use a risky point of view—second person (you) or first-person plural or some other unique approach. Write a few pages in this way. You need not keep going, but it's a good idea to experiment, to explore your options.

PROMPT: Write a chapter or two of a Victorian novel, one that uses an omniscient point of view, in which the author is a god-like voice seeing and knowing everything. Then write a few pages using this approach in the piece you're working on.

PROMPT: Review your recent work to discover which points of view you tend to use and which ones seem to work best for you. Then write a few pages using a different point of view to explore the same material in one of the pieces.

Chapter Nineteen

Western Union

Books about writing tend to avoid the subject of theme. It's a slippery rascal and is so much in the purview of literature courses and so misunderstood as it applies to the writing of narrative, that we usually don't confront it directly. We say that theme is organic, that it grows naturally out of the story itself and to be conscious of it is to risk flagrant didacticism. And those statements have a lot of truth in them. If pressed, we fall back on the famous, if perhaps apocryphal, statement by movie mogul Samuel Goldwyn, who reportedly said that if you want to send a message, you should use Western Union. The statement bristles with the reductive fury that is so simple and reassuring to embrace. Right on, Sammy boy. Damn straight. None of that self-conscious message-sending for us.

But let's you and me take a little time to talk about theme as a source of ideas for storytelling and as a technical element of the craft, one that can help rescue stalled stories. First, a word about what theme *isn't*. It's not the "moral of the story." It can't be wrapped up in a quick sentence imparting some truth like "cheaters never prosper" or "what goes around comes around." It is not The Main Point, as discussed in literature courses. English teachers use the term frequently, often on final exams, asking questions like "What is the theme of *Light in August*?" Using the word "theme" in that way is perfectly acceptable when studying literature. But we're going to talk about theme as it relates to us as the makers of stories.

Theme, as we're discussing it, also is not one of those *man vs. nature,* *man vs. man, man vs. himself* phrases. You know the ones. They're a critical shorthand that can lead us into the study of a work of art, and they serve their purpose in that regard. But we're not particularly interested in a lot of versus-ing at the moment. For us, theme means the abstract, unifying ideas that drive a story, that give it resonance and, for lack of a better word, meaning beyond the specifics of the story's characters and actions. Often that resonance is difficult, even impossible, to articulate in a way that gives it justice. It's a conceptual matter, one that as writers we struggle to capture on the page, though we realize that if we were able to capture it completely it would be destroyed. It would be, to quote T.S. Eliot "not what I meant at all." Or, if you prefer a pop cultural reference, it's what the rock group Pink Floyd pointed to in the lines "The time is gone/the song is over/ thought I'd something more to say." Theme is the something more we have to say.

Critics and writers point to theme by saying a story's theme is "loneliness" or "passing youth" or "family" or "romantic love." It's the concept imbedded in human experience that the story in some way investigates. Your story about a family's struggle to move beyond old grudges and rituals can be said to investigate the theme of "family." Very often these themes rise organically from the story, as mentioned earlier. Nevertheless, it's worthwhile for a writer as she writes to gain a sense of the theme that is rising organically from what she's writing. Through her awareness, she can hone and amplify the theme as the story progresses, using it as a guiding light to discover the story's essence and direction. In short, it can be a source of ideas for developing the story and for getting a stalled story moving again.

Ideas From Theme

If I were coaching a writer on a blocked or unsuccessful story, I wouldn't suggest investigating the theme as the first place to start the revival process. As we've discussed in this section of the book, it's important to look at structure and character, point of view and details. However, don't ignore the possibility of using theme to get a story going again. Writers often miss this option and thereby limit their possibilities for success.

Exploring the themes of past writing also can be helpful. You'll learn about who you are as a writer and how your themes tend to imbed themselves in your work. Our stories often investigate the same theme or themes time and again. Something in our psychological make-up draws us back to a theme or two, even if we're trying consciously to avoid that theme. If you read the stories you've written one after the next, you'll find that a particular theme asserts itself throughout them, even if the stories explore vastly different material. It's quite likely that your funny essay about your first love, your short story about a supernatural grocery clerk, and your novel about a serial killer all share a similar theme—disillusioned idealism, perhaps, or the search for personal identity.

In using theme to build your stories, to add ideas to the generative idea, it's important to reach a point at which you're aware of the themes you're investigating. You'll find them in recurring images, in patterns of character and event. They'll spring from your imagination, your unconscious. I'm not saying you should force them out. I'm saying that after you've written your way into a story, be mindful of what's appearing on the page and look for ways to amplify those patterns.

For example, let's explore the following scenario.

You have an idea for a story and have begun writing it, unsure exactly where you're headed but engaged nonetheless. You've written a few pages, a couple of scenes, descriptions of the characters. The story involves a woman who breeds collies. A childless widow, retired from her job, she dedicates her life to her dogs. She has built elaborate kennels in her backyard, where she keeps a half-dozen dogs from various litters. Her neighbors have begun complaining to her about the constant barking. They want something done about it.

As you develop the story, you are engaged by this character. You've described her in detail, written a history about her in your notebook, sprinkling key moments from that history into the story. You want to write more, but after a couple of scenes in which the neighbors confront her about the noise, you're not sure where to go. What would she do? What are her options? What should happen next? You try a few ideas but nothing seems right. The new scenes don't ring true.

One way to move the story forward is to look at the theme or themes emerging from what you've written. What is the abstract idea driving you to write this story? Who is this character and why does she appeal to you? Do you admire her? Pity her? Which details recur in the pages you've written? The woman's mud-spattered boots, in which she trudges around her yard and cleans the kennels? Or perhaps you've spent several paragraphs describing the kennels themselves, how they're connected by chicken wire, how each dog has a favorite toy on the floor of the kennel. From these details, and the tone in which they're presented, you'll be able to perceive the themes you're exploring. Is this a story about loneliness? A story about the ways we survive loss? Maybe it's a story about the connection between humans and animals, how we help each other to persevere.

With a sense of your theme, even if you can't articulate it, you'll gain a sense of direction, and you can use that direction to build new ideas into the story. Again, I'm not suggesting you reduce your story to a one-sentence capsule. I am suggesting that you be mindful of the patterns emerging from the story and use those patterns to direct you as the story unfolds. For example, you've noticed that the woman's muddy boots are mentioned three or four times. They seem to be linked to the nature of the character. When you see the character in your mind, she's always wearing those boots. You see the boots in your mind when she's not wearing them, when they're standing by the door that leads to the backyard.

Brainstorm new ideas about those boots. Were they a present from her dead husband? Were they a gift to herself upon the husband's death? How do they feel on her feet? Do they pinch the bunion on her left foot, or do they slide on easily, a reassuring element of her daily routine? How can they play a greater role in the story? Do they figure somehow in the ending of the story? If they took a more prominent role, how would the story change?

As we've discussed, writing stories requires a balance between control and letting go, the conscious and the unconscious. This is true especially in regard to theme. We must be aware of our theme and yet not force it. We can use it to foster new ideas, gently guiding the piece forward. Look for theme in your characters—their goals and attitudes, the situations that confront them. Look for theme in the conflicts. Look for theme in the details, the tone, the point of view. Question each of these elements, separately and as they work with each other.

Though some writing teachers might advise against it, you can begin a story with a theme in mind. This approach is more often taken with nonfiction, particularly the essay, but it can be used in fiction, plays, and screenplays too. For example, you could say, "I'm going to write something about ambition. It's a subject I think about a lot. I'm fascinated by the power of ambition to shape a person's life." Begin brainstorming about ambition and see where you go. If you're feeling stuck on a piece, or if you're fiddling around with what to write next, choosing a theme can fire your imagination. Try it.

When taking this approach, however, be sure you're exploring a theme rather than dramatizing a conclusion you've already reached. For example, if you want to investigate the nature of ambition, you could move in many directions and generate a lot of great ideas. But if you've already decided what you think about ambition and are using the story simply to present your conclusions, your story will be limited, your characters mere pawns to those conclusions. For example, if you've already decided that ambition leads to greed and narcissism, all that's left is for you to create a character who enacts that conclusion. The story will seem self-conscious and manipulative. There will be no room for give and take with your reader and no room for your imagination to roam. It will be little more than propaganda for whatever point you've already decided you want to make.

It's far better to explore a concept and allow yourself to be surprised and enlightened by the results on the page. In fact, as writers we often discover what we think about something through the act of writing. I know a number of talented writers of journalism who avoid more creative forms because they "have nothing to say." What they don't realize—or admit—is that writing creatively is the means toward finding out what you "have to say." If you already know exactly what you have to say, there's little point in writing the story.

Breaking Blocks With Theme

In the "lady with the pet dogs" example we've already touched on how theme can supply direction and get your story moving, but let's explore this idea a bit further. If you're blocked on a story, perhaps the reason is that you're being untrue to the essential theme. Therefore, the story rings false to you. You need to go through what you've written and try to discern what theme you're investigating.

One reason you may be off track is because you're pushing the story in a direction it doesn't want to go. In the dog-breeder story, we might be forcing the conflict with the neighbors. We've developed a compelling character and don't know what to do with her. Sometimes putting a story away for a while can help, can give you fresh insights into the story's essence. We can pull it out of the file later and see clearly that the neighbors have nothing to do with the real story. We'd trucked them in to supply conflict, something to push the story forward dramatically. If we conclude, perhaps through our investigation of the boots, that the woman is coping with her own sense of mortality, heightened by the death of her husband, we can shift direction away from the neighbors and focus on other possibilities. Perhaps the conflict should involve the impending death of one of the dogs. Or perhaps the birth of a new litter. Or perhaps a family with young children that arrives to check on the impending birth of a puppy they've bought. Or . . . well . . . lots of things. Now, instead of feeling dry and blocked, we have a number of options to explore. By discovering a sense of the story's theme, new doors have opened.

In the past few weeks I've been thumbing through some story files, ancient ones from years ago. I found one that contained drafts of a story I'd forgotten I'd written—or attempted to write. It concerned a man who frequents an all-night gas station. The station sat on a corner of a busy street in a small town, and featured a rather large, concrete fountain. The man enjoyed ambling to the station at midnight, buying a soda or a candy bar, and sitting next to the fountain. And that's what he did. Unfortunately, that's *all* he did. The station was based on a place near where I was living at the time, and I liked going there. I wanted to write about it. The man in the story wasn't based on me. He was much older, alone, with few prospects in his life. I must have tried a dozen different ways to get a story from him. Never happened. In reading the story recently I realized that I wanted to explore his loneliness and feelings of uncertainty. The station, open all night, provided a small sense of permanence and comfort, something to count on in the dark night of the soul. With those ideas in mind, I hope to return to that story, if it's not too late, and focus on those themes.

Sometimes it takes awhile for the themes to emerge. And sometimes we need to complete a draft of a piece to discover its theme. That discovery, and the opportunities for new ideas that it offers, become part of the revision process. In the first draft we may be focused on getting the story's basic elements in place, developing the characters, moving the plot toward its conclusion, keeping the details sharp and interesting. When the draft is finished, we can investigate what our unconscious minds are trying to tell us through the story. When we discover that essential unifying element, we can revise to bring it to greater prominence. It can inspire no end of new ideas for taking a solid draft and making it into something wonderful.

Questions to Consider

1. What themes permeate the writing you've done in the past? How have you explored these themes? Were you conscious of them as you wrote?

2. Are there themes you've tried to avoid in your writing, ones that are too close to you emotionally? Are you ready to tackle them yet?

3. What themes are you exploring in an ongoing piece? How can you explore theme with greater power, at greater depth?

4. Are you blocked on a piece at the moment? Have you investigated the theme? What might the theme be trying to tell you about the direction of the piece?

Put It On Paper

PROMPT: Read a piece of writing that's been in your dead-end file for a while. Read with an eye toward theme. What themes run through it? Locate where that theme is strongest—a scene, a paragraph of description, even just a phrase or sentence. Using that moment as your core, write a few pages to expand upon it.

PROMPT: As we discussed, theme usually is embedded in patterns—of event, detail, character, tone, setting. Read a piece of writing from your dead-end file and focus on patterns, on things that recur. It may be as simple as the lady's boots in our example. Write a few pages expanding on this pattern. For something like the boots, you could tell their history from the day she bought them.

PROMPT: Pick a dark theme to explore such as death, despair, a loss of some type. In a few pages, write a dramatic scene to explore this theme, but use a light, even humorous, tone.

PROMPT: Spend some time reading work you've completed, at least three pieces. Look for recurring themes. Choose one and begin a new piece with that theme in mind, writing at least a few pages. Explore it in a way you've never tried before. For example, if you've written some short stories with the theme of unrequited love, begin an essay on that subject. Or, if you've dealt with that theme in stories with a somber tone, set out to write a funny story about it.

PROMPT: Pick a theme that interests you and write a page or two of an essay titled "On [your theme]." Now write a page or two in which you explore the theme dramatically in fiction, memoir, or a script. If you want, decide which of the two approaches interests you more, then keep writing.

PROMPT: If you're blocked on a piece, read only the first page. If the piece ended there, what would you say is its theme? Then read the next page and state the theme to that point. Work your way through the piece reading one page at a time. Is the theme consistent? Is it elaborated on? Does it shift and grow muddled? Try to determine what the theme should be and begin writing from there.

PROMPT: Read the jacket of a book you haven't read. You may want to go to your bookstore and pick some at random from the shelves. Back jackets often state the themes of the book. A quick browse of my own shelves led to "a personal journey of the nature of miracles," "reaches for a deeper understanding of fatherhood," "an uplifting story of community," "a story of fearsome sadness." Of course, these phrases are the stuff of sales copy, but they try to find the essence of the books. Pick one phrase that interests you, that suggests a theme of some type, and write a few pages. You might begin, for example, your own "story of fearsome sadness" or your own essay on "fatherhood."

PROMPT: Pluck a character from your notebook, someone you've been itching to write about. Write a few pages—a character sketch, biography, a scene or two. Then read what you've written with an eye toward theme. What do you discover about the character, his or her significance to you in a thematic sense? Can you keep going?

PROMPT: Use an object in your house as the focus of a couple of pages of writing. You might want to place the object on your writing table and describe it, or you could begin a piece with a description of the object. Push on for as long as you can. Don't think about theme or "the point." Don't analyze what you're doing at all. Be content to freewrite, allowing the object to guide you. When you finish, put the piece away for a week and then read it. What patterns emerge—words, images, tone, whatever. What theme does the pattern suggest?

PROMPT: Make a short list of your favorite pieces of writing. Freewrite about the themes of these pieces. Do they share similar themes? Are these the themes you tend to explore in your own work?

Part IV

Better Ideas

Chapter Twenty

Getting Started

In this chapter and the ones that follow in this final section, we'll narrow our focus to putting words on paper. The prompts in this section will help you through the various stages of building a narrative, from getting started to improving a completed draft. I hope that the instructional text in this book has been helpful, but at some point we must put away the books and sit down to write.

The prompts in this chapter will help you begin a project. If you're feeling uninspired, you might find something here that will spark you. If you're feeling inspired but don't know where to start, give a few prompts a try. If you've been blocked for a while, you might find the way to break through that block. If you just want to warm up with an exercise or two, you'll find them here.

Put It On Paper

PROMPT: Make a list of as many aspects of your life as possible, from the big, important stuff to the most inconsequential. The list could include your job, the names of your friends, the make and model of your car, your favorite food, whatever. You won't think of everything at one sitting, so be patient with yourself. Add to the list whenever you think of something. Anything that's an ongoing part of your life, such as "enjoy the smell of tulips," "can't sleep on Sunday nights," "love watching re-runs of *Seinfeld*."

PROMPT: Pull an item or two from the list you made in the previous prompt and write a few pages about it in whatever way seems most natural. You could explore the subject in a personal essay or fictionalize it in some way.

PROMPT: Write about a hobby or avocation that used to play an important role in your life but that no longer is a part of your life.

PROMPT: Find a title in a collection of stories, essays, or plays that you've not read. Write a page of narrative that would fit the title.

PROMPT: Put three characters in a room. Each character thinks the other two are aligned against him or her. Write a dialogue. If you want, write the scene three times, each time from the point of view of a different character.

PROMPT: Write a scene in which a character shows up at an event wearing the wrong type of clothes.

PROMPT: Have you ever had the common dream of showing up too late for something? The most common is a dream about showing up for school too late to take a test, but there are many variations. Usually the dream wakes us with a start. Allow yourself to keep dreaming (on paper, of course) and continue the scenario. How do you, or how does your character, resolve the situation?

PROMPT: Recall a family situation or event that went wrong or turned out badly in some way. Write about what happened, shedding light on the event, or fictionalize it and change the ending—making it either happier or more disastrous.

PROMPT: Write a scene in which some type of sound interrupts (or triggers) a heated discussion. Consider: a barking dog, a ringing telephone, a blaring television, a creaking staircase, a rumbling car, a dripping faucet.

PROMPT: Your character wakes in the morning and goes to a window to see an unlikely animal—a moose, ostrich, or something similar—staring back. What happens?

PROMPT: Explore the cliché "from the mouths of babes." Write about a time in which something a child said made you see something in a new light or inspired you to take some type of action. If you've never had this experience, fictionalize one.

PROMPT: Read the local section of your newspaper every day for a week. If possible, keep the sections in a pile. Choose two stories that interest you and find a way to fuse them into a single situation, then explore it. If possible, bring both elements into a single sentence and use that to begin the story. For example, you might find a story about a house fire and another about an annual Easter egg hunt held in a local park. Your opening sentence could be—"On the day of the annual Easter egg hunt, an event my brothers and sisters wouldn't miss for the world, our house burned to the ground."

PROMPT: Write about a time when someone gave you or someone you know a piece of bad news in an insensitive or inappropriate way. If you want, fictionalize the experience, changing it to fit your needs. Either way, get even with the lout who needs a lesson in manners.

PROMPT: What is your least favorite way to travel? Are you afraid of flying? Do you hate buses? Write about your feelings for this mode of transportation, exploring the reasons you feel this way. If you prefer, send a character who shares your feelings on a trip involving that type of travel.

PROMPT: Make a confession. Come on. You can do it. No one else has to see it. You can burn the pages afterward.

PROMPT: Write a scene in which no one talks. You must convey all the meaning through silent action.

PROMPT: Play a round of creativity roulette. Cut twenty pictures from magazines. Use a variety of magazines, so you'll have lots of tones and subjects. Crumble the pictures into balls and throw them in a box or vase or some type of container. Pick three of the balls and straighten them. Write a few pages involving all three images. One tip: Don't cheat. Use the first three you pick.

PROMPT: As writers we're told time and again that we must hook our readers with the first paragraph. To that end, we try to open in a dramatic or surprising way. Try the opposite approach. Open with a character sitting and thinking quietly.

P R O M P T : Open with a character saying he or she is the world's greatest something. It could be something the character brags about—world's greatest softball player or world's greatest decorator. Or it could be something said in a self-deprecating way—world's greatest whiner or world's greatest spoiler of a fun evening. Then have the character tell an anecdote to support his or her claim.

P R O M P T : Describe a place you know, or one you imagine, by focusing on smells and sounds. Continue your description until a person or fictional character appears, then shift the focus to the character. Then introduce a second person or character. Keep going.

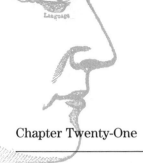

Chapter Twenty-One

Adding Ideas

We've talked at some length about the importance of adding ideas to your initial idea to complicate and expand your premise. In this chapter you'll find prompts to help you do that. I'll assume you have an idea for a piece and have developed it in at least a page of writing, probably more than a page. You may have written your way through the initial burst of inspiration and are unsure how to move forward. Or, you may have explored the initial idea in a limited way and are looking for ways to develop the idea. Or, you may have begun with a burst of inspiration, but you've hit a creative wall. You're not only unsure how to proceed, you're feeling blocked.

The prompts in this chapter speak to all of those situations. Use them for those reasons but keep them, and the thinking behind them, for this stage of any project you begin in the future. With these prompts, and all the prompts in the book, feel free to add or alter the instruction in a way that suits the particulars of the piece you have in progress.

Put It On Paper

PROMPT: Qualify or contradict a statement that you or a character made in the opening pages. For example, if your character claims to be content with the life he's chosen, have him explain what he means and add a note of doubt.

PROMPT: Add a new piece of information about a character or person who appears in the opening pages, a piece of information that contradicts or amplifies the reader's understanding of the character. For example, if the opening focuses on observations about your mother and her lack of tact, tell the reader something that characterizes her in a different light.

PROMPT: Adjust the tone of the piece by adding a different note. If, for example, your opening is loaded with high-energy drama, shift to a quieter mood, for at least a paragraph. If your opening is somber, add a sentence or two of humor.

PROMPT: Add a new element to a relationship. If your pair of detectives have been focused on news about a case, suggest—or state—that they were romantically involved at an earlier time. If your character is struggling with a tyrannical boss, for example, make the boss an old rival from high school or a distant relative.

PROMPT: If you know what comes next in your piece but can't seem to build the bridge to get there, skip to that part, jamming it right up against what you've already written.

PROMPT: Add a new person to the piece. If you've been focused on two characters in a situation, for example, bring in a third. Allow that character to change the personal dynamic in some way, entering with his or her own agenda. For example, if your memoir of a family picnic has focused on you and your brother, show us what Uncle Dave is doing over there on the volleyball court.

P R O M P T : If you're writing a memoir or personal essay, say something that surprises you about the subject you're exploring. Or, if you're feeling nervy, say something that reveals a detail about you or deeper feelings about the subject.

P R O M P T : Slow the pace at which you're introducing characters or people. We sometimes move too quickly in the early pages, feeling we must get the piece moving as fast as possible. Take time to linger, giving the reader a richer beginning.

P R O M P T : Shift the narrative mode. If you've begun with a page of description to present the setting, move right into a scene. If you've explained the situation and presented the background information, move to the present time of the story. If you've begun with a scene, move to narrative summary. If you've begun with characters speaking, move into the mind of a character and present his thoughts.

P R O M P T : Make a general statement or have a character make one—a sweeping statement, along the lines of "people always work to undermine their own best interests," or "Jill will never be a happy person as long as she keeps dating engineers." It should be a statement that adds a new tone or moves the piece in a new direction. By that I mean, the first scene might have shown Jill coming home aglow from a first date with a man she met recently.

P R O M P T : Add a seemingly unrelated object, one that comes quickly to mind (and therefore probably has some connection in your unconscious mind to the piece). For example, if you've been discussing how your lover left abruptly, introduce the potted corn plant standing next to your front window.

P R O M P T : Ask a question. Or have a character ask a question. Surprise yourself and just write one down. Even if the question seems unrelated to what has come before, follow it, find out where it goes or where the answer to the question (or the lack of an answer or the struggle to answer) takes you.

P R O M P T : Shift the time. If you've opened with a night scene, take us to the next afternoon. If you've opened in the present, shift us back to 1972.

P R O M P T : If you know what comes next but can't seem to build the bridge to get there, change course, inventing or choosing a new direction.

P R O M P T : Shift the character's goal. In an earlier chapter we discussed ways to use a character's goal to structure a story. Your opening probably makes clear this goal, either directly or indirectly. Write a page in which the character is not focused at all on achieving this goal. If you're writing a memoir and you've focused on coming to terms with an experience in your past, nudge yourself away from this focus.

P R O M P T : Add a second thread. If the opening of your novel concerns the theft of a priceless painting, move to a bar where customers argue about the chances of the Red Sox winning the pennant. If your opening concerns a woman walking home from a job interview and worrying about money, have her stop at a grocery and concentrate on finding fresh oranges for her kids. In her essay "That's What Dogs Do," Amy Hempel opens with a brief discussion on why she writes, then adds a second element, her attempts to train her dog.

PROMPT: Sustain the action of the opening scene. If you planned to end at a certain spot and move to flashback or summary, stay focused on what happens next in the dramatic present and maintain your focus, even if you're not sure where you're headed.

PROMPT: Show your character doing something uncharacteristic. For example, your soft-spoken accountant could fold a wad of bills from the petty cash drawer into his pocket. Or, you may want to show that your character doesn't perceive herself in the way others perceive her. Isaac Singer's Gimpel, in the short story "Gimpel the Fool" is often bullied and manipulated by those around him. They think he's a fool. But he sees himself much differently, and his voice in the story has a quality of strength.

PROMPT: Change the atmosphere. If your opening is light and straight-forward, add a note of eeriness. If your story opens in a silent, empty house, shift the scene to a carnival full of crowds, noise, and excitement.

PROMPT: Shift the setting. If you've opened at the family picnic, shift to a new location. If you've described the sun rising against a cityscape, move us inside to a diner for breakfast.

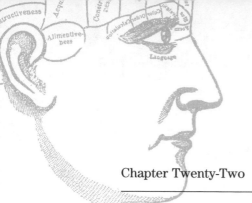

Chapter Twenty-Two

Stuck in the Middle

One of the worst times for a writer is when a project has been moving along for a good while and then stops moving. We've made a commitment to the piece and spend much time and effort developing it to this point. Try as we might, we can take it no further. We curse and fret, enjoy an occasional moment of false promise, then find ourselves struggling again.

As I mentioned earlier in the book, a struggle is a natural part of the process. There's a truism about this struggle that you've probably heard: Writin' is fightin'. But when a piece is going well, we win the fights, or at least most of them. When it's going bad, we're always on our backs, a striped-shirted referee counting us out or asking us how many fingers he's holding up.

The reasons for shutting down in the middle are varied. We lose our energy or interest in the project. We've grown bored with it. Or we've written ourselves into a corner and feel we have no way to get the piece moving again. The direction and nature of the piece inevitably changes as we write, and we might be confused about shape and direction the piece is telling us to take. We may have taken an unfortunate turn early in the piece, the results of which confound us.

Sometimes the block is linked to our non-writing lives. Pressures from our jobs or families sap the energy we had been reserving for our creative work. We're struggling with a crisis. Or sometimes we're having too much fun and don't want to retreat into the solitude of writing. We've gotten out of the habit of writing. Scott Fitzgerald struggled for years with the novel that became *Tender Is the Night*, squandering his talent on the high life in the south of France, then struggling with Zelda's breakdown and his own alcoholism. His writer's block had little to do with writing.

If you're stuck in the middle of a project, consider what's happening in your life and observe if some new situation is sapping your energy and creative drive. If not, if the problem is on the page, then try some of the prompts in this chapter and get yourself moving again. One caveat: Don't fight the prompts. If you've been stuck in the middle for awhile you're probably feeling frustrated, even helpless. Your impulse might be to read a prompt and think *"That* won't work." Take the leap of faith and give them a try.

Put It On Paper

PROMPT: Read what you've written so far, highlighting the lines and the sections that are working well. Try to determine what quality these parts possess, such as humor or insight or an energy in the voice. Notice if you find yourself highlighting fewer parts as the pages progress. In the next page that you write, don't focus as much on what happens as on bringing that quality or qualities back into the piece.

PROMPT: If you haven't already, determine your destination in the piece, not so much the final conclusion you hope to draw as where you plan to end in terms of time and place. In your mind, or on a piece of paper, draw a line between where you are now and where you want to be at the end. You may want to outline the steps you'll need to take to reach your destination. If you don't like outlines, write down your thoughts about how to get to where you want to go. Then write one page that moves you a bit further toward your destination, a page that takes the next step, so to speak. Then write another.

PROMPT: As an alternative to the previous prompt, read what you've written so far, keeping in mind the destination you've noted. Is this really your destination? Sometimes we begin writing with a particular destination, goal, or purpose in mind, but as we've discussed, a creative project will assert a will of its own. The destination for the piece you're developing may have changed, and your efforts to push toward the old one could block you. It may be time to determine a new destination or, scary as it sounds, write for a while without a destination in mind.

PROMPT: Once again, and especially if you haven't done so already, read what you've written so far. Often writers frustrate themselves by focusing on the next step when they're blocked. They try a number of options, sending the piece in one direction, then another, but nothing seems to work. The problem might be that they're focused on the wrong spot in the piece. The problem doesn't reside in the pages they wrote right before they began to feel blocked. The problem resides in an earlier passage. For various reasons, the problem didn't assert itself fully on the piece until later. Read your piece with an eye toward a wrong move, a shift that may have seemed natural at the time but upon close reading pushes the piece toward an inevitable block.

PROMPT: Sometimes we need to leap out of the middle and go to the end. Spend a session or two sketching your ending. If you feel comfortable and confident, write the ending. Then, with that ending in mind, return to the middle and begin writing toward the ending you've completed already.

PROMPT: Put the piece away for a specific, short period of time. Dive right into something new. Don't even miss a single session. Concentrate on the new piece. The distraction can release the block on the other piece.

PROMPT: A variation on the previous prompt: Put the piece away for a specific period of time but make it a longer period than the previous one. But do give yourself a deadline. Otherwise, you could drift away and never finish.

PROMPT: With a long project, we can fall into a rut, moving in an uninspired way through our paces. This feeling also can occur with shorter projects that are protracted by interruptions. We lose the zest of the initial inspiration. If you're stuck in this way, go back to the beginning and spend some time reading the first pages, trying to recapture some of that early energy. You may find yourself editing a bit, changing lines and words, adding some details.

PROMPT: Add a surprising element—surprising to you as well as to your reader. It could be a small detail or a significant announcement. The point is that it gives you something new and something you didn't expect. When we're blocked we sometimes hammer on the same spot, trying new approaches that really are variations on the same approach. It may be time to step back and reconceive the piece.

PROMPT: The writer Philip Gerard once told me "You're not really revising until you cut something that hurts." It may be time to do that in order to free yourself from the blocked middle. Review what you've written, looking for a turn or a passage that you like but that doesn't serve the piece. Often this is a passage in which we're pleased with ourselves, one that involves some type of cleverness or showing off. The passage makes us feel like geniuses. It calls attention to us and to itself.

If it doesn't serve the piece, however, it needs to go. It could be causing the block that's holding up your momentum.

PROMPT: Sometimes a narrative thread isn't so much tangled as frayed. We've grown a bit tired of it. Our energy and enthusiasm have flagged. In this case, look for a spot in the piece that does interest you, even if it plays a minor role in the grand plan. Explore it for awhile. It could end up playing a larger role, or it may renew your interest in the piece as a whole.

PROMPT: If you've been working intuitively on the piece to this point, following its development on faith rather than on a clear notion of your intentions, it may be time to stop and review what you've done so far. Working intuitively, allowing a piece to develop of its own accord, is a fine way to work, as we've discussed throughout this book. But as we write in this way, we can't help but make certain conclusions about it. We can't help but begin to sense its nature and direction. Perhaps your sense of the piece needs adjustment. As you read it, try to put out of your mind the conclusions you've drawn and allow yourself to find fresh clues. Your unconscious mind has planted them, and they're waiting to be discovered.

PROMPT: If you've been working from an outline, it may be time to assess your plan. An outline can be an effective tool for keeping us on track, but we must be willing to revise it as the project develops. It's difficult to know what a story will reveal to us before we've begun writing it. Adhering too closely to an outline developed at the start can lead to blocks when the piece is underway. As you review your outline, look for ways to revise it that will create possibilities for moving forward.

PROMPT: At a writers group meeting I overheard a guy say, "I've written the first half of three novels." He went on to admit that, although he'd been writing for years, he'd yet to finish a novel. He probably had specific reasons why each project stalled and could explain them in detail. But clearly there's a pattern at work in his writing life that is undermining his success. If you find yourself facing a similar pattern, it's time to step back and evaluate what's stopping you. Rather than focus on the particulars of the blocked project, try to recognize the pattern of not completing projects. Some projects are better left uncompleted, as we discussed in section one. However, if project after project ends up in the dead-end file, there's a problem. We can't begin to cover all the psychological possibilities for such a pattern right now, but I highly advise spending time to explore those tendencies on your own. Focusing on the latest block, when many have preceded it, would be fruitless. Take some time to explore—in your mind and also on paper—the pattern of half-finished projects. Write about it at length.

PROMPT: Write your characters' names on strips of paper and put the strips into a container. At the start of the next writing session pick a strip and focus the session on that character. Don't feel as if you have to write about that character within the context of the stalled project. You could write an unrelated sketch or scene involving the character. The point is to return to a free-spirited sense of play. A project, as we all know, can begin with inspiration and exhilaration, then turn into a grind. This is particularly true of long projects. After a while, they can lose their energy. We eventually stop writing, not because we're blocked on the piece so much as we're exhausted with it. That exhaustion, however, can feel like a block. To get yourself going again, return to that sense of play. This prompt and the next ones offer ways to do that.

PROMPT: Place two characters who don't share a scene in the ongoing project into a scene. Have them meet and discuss the conflict at the heart of this project. Buy them a few drinks or find some other way to induce them to speak candidly. If you want, insert yourself into the scene, explaining your problems in writing the piece.

PROMPT: Spend a session writing about your setting. Do a little research and write a brief history of the place. If it's a fictional place, write a brief fictional history.

PROMPT: Brainstorm a list of possibilities of what happens next in the piece. Be as imaginative and illogical as possible. Risk some flights of fancy. Don't worry that you would have to change what you've written already to allow for these possibilities to be, well, possible. Have fun with it.

PROMPT: Take your block to Writer's Block Anonymous. Surround yourself with your favorite writers, and create a scene in which you explain your block and seek their advice.

PROMPT: Interview yourself about the block. We discussed this approach in section one as a way of generating ideas for a project. Use it at this stage to get ideas for moving past the block. Your interviewer should be ruthlessly insistent, continuing to probe for answers, even if you're resistant or confused. Your interviewer shouldn't be chiding or deprecating. He or she isn't giving you the third degree. However, he or she definitely is seeking answers to the questions.

PROMPT: Pick a word from the dictionary by opening to a page at random and dropping your finger onto a word. Use that word as part of the next sentence you write. Draw the remainder of the paragraph from that sentence. If you're stuck for the next paragraph, choose another word in the same manner.

Chapter Twenty-Three

Stuck at the End

You've made it through the middle and can see the end in sight. You're happy, for the most part, with how the piece has developed. And then you hit a block. You may find yourself struggling with the best way to end the piece, to pull together the narrative threads. Perhaps you made some changes in the middle, and now the ending you had foreseen no longer is appropriate. Questions have been raised that the planned ending doesn't resolve. Perhaps the block occurred when you wrote the planned ending, which had seemed wonderful in your mind but doesn't work on the page. You need a different ending.

There are many reasons why we get stuck at the end. Endings are tough. They may be the toughest stage of the process. In all the earlier stages we can assume we'll resolve problems of character, structure, design, or whatever at some later time. Endings don't offer that luxury. Not only must problems be faced directly and immediately, all those earlier problems to be solved later have come home to roost. *Later* is *now*. We also tend to put a lot of pressure on our endings. We want them to be brilliant. We want to hit the perfect note that will move the reader in a powerful way. If we're writing a humor piece, we want the ending to be hilarious. If we're writing a darker piece, we want the reader to embrace our depth of feeling or profundity of thought. We want the ending to resonate. In short, we want the ending to be perfect. With those goals in our minds, it's no wonder we have such a tough time with endings.

As I mentioned in the previous chapter, we also might be suffering writer's block for reasons that have nothing to do with writing. The blocked ending results from stress about your job or a relationship, about money, about dozens of other things that affect our lives. Or you may be undergoing some personal transition, and for the moment lack clarity and direction in your life, and therefore have little to offer your writing. The prompts in this chapter assume the problem is on the page, and so we won't deal with these personal reasons, but they're worth considering as you try to move through the block.

Put It On Paper

PROMPT: Sometimes we're blocked at the end because the endings we've written don't satisfy the expectations we've raised in the reader's mind. To satisfy those expectations, you have to know what they are. Read the piece with an eye toward the expectations you've raised. What implicit promise have you made to the reader throughout the piece? Finding the killer? Requiting the love? Bringing the protagonist to a new level of insight about a situation? Apprentice writers in workshops and groups often say "I liked the story except for the ending." This sends the writer of the piece back to the ending for revision and may block the writer. The problem is not necessarily in the ending. It lies earlier in the piece, when expectations were raised unintentionally in the reader's mind. Find that spot and begin revising there.

PROMPT: Perhaps the problem lies in the pressure you're putting on the ending. Read the final four or five paragraphs. Do you need them all? Perhaps your piece will end more naturally if you cut the last paragraph or two. When you wrote these paragraphs you weren't conscious of their need to wow the reader. They probably possess a simplicity that can work well to end the piece.

PROMPT: In endings we sometimes shift from *show* to *tell*. We want to sum up the piece, to tell the reader what he or she is supposed to think. If the endings you've written, and rejected, take this approach, shift to dramatic mode. End with some type of action.

PROMPT: If you've ended with an action, perhaps it's too final, too close-ended. You can't find the resonance you seek because that action stops the reader with a bang. Open up the ending by using an ongoing action, along the lines of "We got back in the car and began driving toward Denver, using the Rockies in the distance as our guide." Though surely your ending will be more graceful than this example of driving off into the sunset, it shows characters in motion. It suggests a possible future rather than abruptly slamming a door on the narrative.

PROMPT: To extend our discussion in the previous prompt, consider that your ending may be too pat. Its simplicity undercuts the thematic layers of the piece. For example, a writer has developed a personal essay about her struggle with bulimia, in which she investigates the sources of the problem, its manifestations, and the ways it affected her life. To pull the piece together at the end she offers a reductive statement about life being a learning experience or "what doesn't kill us makes us stronger." Readers complain that the ending is unsatisfying, or the writer senses that it's not quite right, though she's not sure why. The reason it fails to satisfy is that she has treated the experience with thought-provoking sophistication that the ending doesn't match. She's created an expectation in the reader's mind of a thought-provoking, sophisticated conclusion but hasn't delivered it. In her attempt to end with a quick summing up, she has not done justice to her theme.

PROMPT: Perhaps the problem with the ending is one of focus. I read many stories for workshops and conferences that shift away from the protagonist or the main conflict at the end. The writer pulls back to give some universal insight about life and the human condition. If you've taken this approach, put the focus back on the central character or situation.

PROMPT: The problem may be a matter of tone. At a recent conference I read a story about a woman's attempts to meet a man. The story was witty and sharp, with a light note of despair that added dimension. Then, in the last few paragraphs, the light note erupted like a bomb, changing the tone in a way that jarred the reader. The writer hadn't prepared the reader. If your ending suffers from such a shift, you can either change the ending to fit the earlier tone or foreshadow the shift by modulating the tone throughout the piece, dipping into the darker tone from time to time, so that when it appears in full force at the end the reader has been prepared.

PROMPT: Maybe you feel that the ending doesn't unify the piece. The easiest way to remedy this problem is to return to a key image or two from earlier in the piece. You might also return to a line of dialogue or recall some earlier event. By returning to these earlier elements, you bring a sense of wholeness to the piece, creating a resonance that ties the piece together.

PROMPT: If you're concerned that the ending is too open, that it doesn't supply enough closure, see the previous prompt. By recalling an element from earlier in the piece, you give the reader a sense of having come "full circle." Of course, you'll need to choose the right element to recall. It needs to be one central to the intention or meaning of the piece—not necessarily the one on which you lavished the most attention when it appeared earlier but one that speaks to the core themes.

PROMPT: One way to circumnavigate the temptation to over-think your ending or overwhelm it with rhetorical flourish is to set a technical challenge for yourself. Decide you're going to end with a line of dialogue. Or with a gesture. Or a description of an object. Or anything else that occurs to you. Choose something appropriate to the piece, of course, but the key point to the exercise is to find a way to end in a natural way with whatever you choose. By concentrating on the challenge of the exercise, you'll free yourself from concentrating too much on perfecting the ending. Straining for perfection may be blocking you.

PROMPT: Read the first few paragraphs of your piece. They may hold the key to your ending. In them you suggested—explicitly or implicitly—the direction of your piece. You pointed the reader to the path that leads to the final paragraphs. The technique of returning directly to the opening is a bit shopworn, and though it still may work I'm not suggesting you be so obvious in your approach. After reading the first paragraphs a few times, and, as best you can, putting out of your mind the piece that developed from them, decide on where the opening would lead. In other words, given this opening, where would the piece inevitably end? Use that marker as the basis for your decision on where you now must end the piece. Perhaps you haven't reached the end, and that's why you're blocked. Perhaps the ending doesn't offer a suitable destination for the opening as it stands, in which case you can either change the opening or write a more suitable ending.

PROMPT: Let's look at another way to use the beginning to find the ending. Read the first few paragraphs looking for ways to echo them in the ending. The technique of returning directly to the beginning in the ending has been done so often and continues to be done in workmanlike nonfiction that I'm not suggesting you do it. Instead, look for more subtle ways to echo the opening. Is there a word you can repeat, an implied question you can answer, a tone you can bring back, a method you can use again? For example, did you open with a statement? A line of dialogue? A quip? An anecdote? A character's thoughts? A description? Use the same approach to end the piece. The reader won't be conscious of what you're doing but will feel a sense of closure on an unconscious level.

PROMPT: Have you considered that you might be blocked by the ending because you're not ready to end? If you're writing genre fiction and the plot has climaxed—the lovers united, the killer caught, the villains vanquished—you're probably sure it's time to wrap up, but if you're writing a piece less dependent on plot, perhaps you're not happy with the ending or are unsure how best to end the piece now because there is more to say. Spend a few sessions pushing beyond the point where you decided to end and find out what happens. Many writers, myself included, have written a short story but struggled with the ending because the ending opened more doors than it closed. And so we were off on a novella or a novel. I wrote a novella in graduate school, bringing the piece to a rousing conclusion that I'd planned early in the process. When I reached that point I realized that the scene pushed the protagonist into a deeper conflict than the conflict that had driven the piece from the start. I struggled for a while to enlarge and deepen the scene, to give it a stronger closure, but the new conflict kept asserting itself. I realized in time that my struggle with the ending was really a struggle against the piece itself and against the realization that I would have to commit to a longer project. Consider that possibility.

PROMPT: Read the endings of ten published pieces in whatever form you're working. You need not read the entire piece. Study the endings as self-contained pieces, trying to determine the technique the author is using. Experiment with several of the techniques—dialogue, statement, thoughts, action, detail, or whatever—applying the particulars of your own piece.

PROMPT: Shift the goal of your ending. If you're trying to end with a quiet gesture, try a sharper, more abrupt approach. If you're trying to end with a summary of the character and events, take a more dramatic approach. In short: Do something different, even the opposite, of what you've been trying to do. We can suffer tunnel vision in trying to make our endings work, limiting our possibilities and leading ourselves into a block.

PROMPT: If you're stuck on what happens in the end, in terms of plot or event, spend the next five session exploring five alternatives. Make each different from the others in a significant way. Tell yourself you're not going to choose from among them until you finish all five.

PROMPT: If you're stuck on what happens in the end, in terms of plot or event, chart the actions and events that occur in the piece to the point where you're blocked. If it helps, make an outline of the piece as it stands so far. Study the outline or sequence or whatever you've done to strip away the other elements of the story. Is there a natural, interesting, compelling flow to the events? Is there a logical system in place? If the answer is no, then the problem isn't the ending. It's what has come before. If the answer is yes, extend the outline to include the next logical event. You may have found your ending. If that event leads to others, you're not yet ready to end the piece.

PROMPT: If the problem is one of resolving a question of character, use the method in the previous prompt, but apply it to character. Strip away the other story elements and determine if you've developed the character and his or her conflict in the way you intended or a way that pleases you. Perhaps your character needs more time on the page, and in your imagination, before you're ready to end.

PROMPT: Consider the draft complete and move to a new piece, setting a deadline for when you're going to return to the current piece for revision. During the time away, try not to focus on resolving the ending. Know that you have more work to do but move your conscious mind away from the struggle for solutions. Your unconscious mind will continue to play with ideas, and the ending will come.

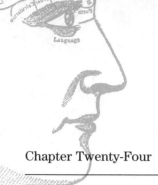

Chapter Twenty-Four

When You're Stuck in Revision

Unless you're working on one of your first pieces, you've probably had the experience of writing a draft, and after finishing it, feeling that it's not the piece you had hoped to write. To some extent, every project has a bit of that feeling. Against the hard black-and-white reality of the page we struggle to place our visions, and rare is the time when the result equals our initial passion and inspiration. Of course, if we did succeed, we might quit writing, so let's try to perceive the struggle as a positive force in our lives.

We'll accept that a finished piece won't quite equal the piece we conceived in our minds at the start. Some pieces, however, will be closer than others. In this chapter, we'll focus on those pieces that fall considerably short. We have a completed draft that somewhere, somehow went wrong, and yet we remain intrigued by its possibilities. There are passages that are very good, and we don't want to lose them. We want to find a way to resurrect those passages that are not yet working.

When you find yourself facing this challenge, as we discussed in an earlier chapter, don't despair. It is part of the writer's life. All writers face it. It doesn't mean you're untalented or a failure. Don't give in to such despair. Successful writers develop a level of resilience that allows them to persevere, to accept the good news—and good stories—with the bad. Cultivating resilience takes time. It's rooted in experience and in perspective, in the ability to see each piece you write as just one of an ongoing development of your art. Some projects come easily, gifts from the muse that appear almost miraculously on the page. Other projects, no matter how hard we try, will not be tamed. Despite wonderful ideas and inspired passages, they never quite work. Some remain unfinished and will remain that way, awaiting our return like the toys of childhood. Others will succeed because we have the fortitude to persist. We work on those pieces with a mixture of tenacity, ambition, frustration, invention, and blind faith. If you're ready to apply that mixture to your completed draft, try some of the prompts below.

Put It On Paper

PROMPT: If you've finished the draft recently—within the past week or two—put it away. Try not to think about it. Your frustration with it might be simply the post-partum depression we often feel after finishing a draft we've worked on for a while. The elation that drove us to write the piece has passed. Our belief that we have written a masterpiece has curdled into the belief that we're nothing more than a self-deluded failure. The piece sucks. It's terrible. Who are we kidding to think we can write anything worth reading? Sound familiar? These feelings tell you that you can't see the piece clearly yet. It may not be the masterpiece you hoped it would be, but those feelings are the result of the loss of elation you used to finish it. Accept this drop in enthusiasm as a natural part of the process. When it has passed, when you find yourself thinking of new ideas or itching to tinker, it's time to read the piece with a fresh vision.

PROMPT: Be willing to start over. If you're committed to making the piece work, nothing can be sacred. You must be willing to let go of all of it. When you achieve this mindset, question the largest issues, such as the structure of the piece, its voice and protagonist. Make a list of several alternatives for every major element. For example, think of three or four distinctively different ways of structuring the piece. Think of several other characters who could be the protagonist.

PROMPT: Commit yourself to at least one significant revision of the piece. In his classic book *Fiction Writer's Workshop*, Josip Novakovich makes a keen observation about how computers have changed the way writers revise. He notes that writers were willing to make larger revisions when they were forced to retype their pieces. Now that computers spare us that drudgery, we tend to tinker with the first draft rather than recast it. There are many advantages to working on a computer, but if you have a serious concern about how well a piece is working, taking time to retype it could lead to the larger revision it may need.

PROMPT: Spend a session writing about the piece. As we've done in earlier prompts, you could do this one as an interview with yourself, framing it in a question-and-answer format. Address your concerns about the piece. Why do you feel it's not working? What seems to be missing? What *is* working? If you can, express your intentions of the piece when you began writing it. Try to capture the essence of the piece in its current state. Compare your intentions with the results and ask yourself how they differ.

PROMPT: Spend a session writing the history of the piece, its evolution from initial idea to its current state. Read what you've written about the piece with an eye toward significant turns or changes. For example, I struggled off and on for several years with a story involving an eccentric character based on someone I met in real life. In early drafts I made him the story's narrator, but his voice overwhelmed the piece. And his eccentricities were such that he was a character who was easier to take at a distance. I switched to third person, but there was still too much of him. I invented a son and told the story through the son's viewpoint, gaining the distance the story needed and making the father more sympathetic. I continued to revise and felt I'd found the answer. After finishing the story, I still wasn't happy with it. For some reason it just didn't work or, rather, it didn't approximate my original hopes for the story. After putting the story away for awhile, working on it from time to time, I mapped its evolution and realized that by introducing the son I had moved too far from the character who most interested me. I had made it a story of fathers and sons rather than one about a man's self-destructive tendencies. Though I was loath to do it, I moved the focus back to that man, subordinating the son. The story regained some of its early magic, and the most compelling character was back at the center again. Having viewed that character through the son's eyes during those drafts, he had grown more sympathetic and more human to me, and so the time spent on those drafts wasn't wasted. By charting the story's evolution, I could see where I'd taken a turn that turned it into a different story, one that didn't possess the wallop of invention that I wanted.

P R O M P T : Read the piece aloud and, if possible, record yourself. Play the tape several times, listening for passages that work and those that don't. Take notes as you listen, scribbling any thoughts and impressions that occur to you. If the sound of your own voice on tape makes you squirm with self-consciousness, ask someone to read the piece aloud to you, and record the reading.

P R O M P T : As a variation on the previous prompt, tell the story to someone rather than reading it directly from the page. Use the same basic structure you used in the written version—including flashbacks, asides, etc.—but don't strive to use the same words you've written. You're trying to gain a sense of the story's logic and clarity, its interest. Does your reader laugh? Cry? Is your reader confused by parts of the story? By telling it in this way you'll gain objectivity, and you'll be able to gauge more clearly your own grasp of the story.

P R O M P T : Distill the draft to its essence by summing it up in one sentence. You may want to sum up in a paragraph and condense the paragraph to a sentence. This process won't be easy, and even after you have your one-sentence statement you may feel you've not done justice to the piece. But the exercise will force you to consider the fundamental nature of the piece. If you aren't able to arrive at some type of statement, perhaps the problem with the draft is that you're not sure yet what you're trying to accomplish in it.

P R O M P T : Sometimes starting small can lead you back into the story. Look for small changes you can make. They can help you past feelings of frustration and failure that block you from seeing the possibilities for improving the story. Spend the next few sessions focused on the little things, telling yourself that you'll confront the larger ones later. For now, fix a line of dialogue, sharpen a description, correct errors in grammar, punctuation, and spelling.

P R O M P T : If the piece is based on a real-life experience, check to be sure you've captured that experience, if you're writing nonfiction. Are all the key elements on the page? Have you evoked the experience sharply enough for a reader to share your thoughts and feelings about it? Add one more element about the experience that, for whatever reason, you chose to exclude in the draft.

PROMPT: If you're writing fiction based on a real-life experience, have you moved the experience far enough from its real-life inspiration that you feel free to change and edit the parts that don't work? Add one more element to the story, an element that is entirely fictional. Your problem with the draft could be that the piece hangs in an awkward middle ground between a self-contained fictional story and your memory of the real-life experience.

PROMPT: Spend a session focused on characters, asking yourself questions about them. Are they compelling? Sympathetic? Are the events in the piece meaningful and significant to the characters? How many characters appear in the piece—write down all the names. Are there too many characters? Too few? Should several characters be condensed into one? Which characters interest you most? Why? Which ones interest you least? Why? What qualities do the characters share? How are they different? Do you know the characters well enough? Are all aspects of the characters on the page or do some remain vague? Are they all described? Are they all described in the same way or do you vary your methods of presenting them? What is the goal of each character in the story?

PROMPT: Spend a session introducing a new character. Describe the character. Use him or her in a scene. How would the piece change if you inserted this character into it?

PROMPT: Check your scenes. How many do you present and how long is each one? Have you varied the length? Are the scenes generally long or short? Is the length of each scene appropriate to its significance to the piece? If you had to cut a scene which one would you cut? Spend a session writing a new scene. How does the scene affect the piece?

PROMPT: Check the pace of the piece. Does it move quickly or slowly? Have you modulated the pace, creating a pleasing rhythm? Is the pace appropriate to the content of the piece? Does it match your intentions when you began writing the piece?

PROMPT: Check the structure of the piece. Do you offer a pleasing mix of scene and summary? Have you provided clear transitions between scenes, chapters, and sections? To do this one, you'll need a printed copy of the piece. Lay the pages across a table so you can see them all. Highlight scene and summary. Use a different color for transitions.

PROMPT: Add a new sentence to every page. If it's a short piece, add a new sentence to every paragraph. You can cut the ones you don't like at a later time. For now, you're trying to extend. Go wild. Push your imagination.

PROMPT: Reverse the previous prompt. Rather than adding sentences, cut a sentence from every page or every paragraph. Determine what has been lost and what has been gained. Put back only those sentences that add something important to the piece.

PROMPT: Add a specific "fact" to every page. If you've described an office to set up a scene, for example, add a fact about that office—the barely perceptible hum of fluorescent lights in the ceiling, the year it was built, the color of the carpet. If you're writing nonfiction, you may have to do some research or test your memory.

PROMPT: Add a detail, trait, or quality to every character, preferably one that enlarges or makes the character more vivid and complex. Don't neglect even minor characters. If the guy from room service appears only for a sentence, to deliver a bottle of champagne, add some stains to his uniform or give him an odd accent.

PROMPT: Spend a few sessions pushing the language. Read each sentence with an eye toward making the language more interesting and more vivid, more particular and specific. Your concern with the draft may not have anything to do with the big elements, such as character or structure. Instead, you may be sensing at some level that the language is uninspired or that it's merely competent. Force yourself to improve a sentence in every paragraph. Look for language that is vague or dull. Make it sparkle.

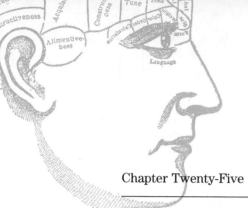

Chapter Twenty-Five

Beginning Again

O ne of the great moments in the writer's life occurs when we declare a piece finished. If it's a short piece, the writer has lived with it for weeks, maybe months. If it's a longer work, the process may take years. As we've discussed throughout this book, writing can be a struggle. Finishing a piece may require starting over several times, cutting long passages of a draft that was fundamentally flawed. Finishing a piece usually includes a handful of turning points when the piece reveals itself and sets the writing in motion in an exciting new direction. The process can require dozens of revisions. It can mean putting the piece away to simmer for a while, then pulling it out and starting work with a fresh eye and spirit. When all the big blocks are in place and the tough early drafts are complete, the writer begins editing and refining. New little bursts of inspiration create interesting details and language. We polish and we polish and we polish. And then, we're finished.

And then, we must begin again.

As a writer you probably know this feeling. You've just finished spending weeks, even months, in the editing and polishing phase of a piece whose larger issues have been resolved long ago. In the final stages you've watched a good piece improve at the micro-level. You've worked with the confidence gained by having spent so much time in the world of the piece. You can flip to the passages you like best, the ones that came from hours of work or were born from a flash of inspiration at four in the morning.

When the work is finished, and the piece is off in the mail to agents or editors, we must return to face the blank page again. Though the prospect of working with new material can be exciting, it also can be a little scary. The confidence of the previous weeks evaporates. You face the unknown. The victories, large and small, of the previous piece mean little now because a new piece sprawls before us.

Many writers feel blocked at this time. It's a natural feeling. Sometimes we slide into a post-partum depression, or a similar psychological state, and lack the energy and will to start anew. As we were writing the previous piece, the one that now stands so lovely and complete, we were concocting the next one. In fact, we had to fight the urge to dive right into it. But now that we don't have to fight the urge anymore, we don't feel the urge anymore. The piece that shimmered like candy in the distance—"I can't wait to start that one!"—seems far less shimmering. We want to keep writing the finished one, to stay in that world.

The prompts in this chapter address the time in our writing lives after we've finished a piece but struggle to begin again. As a general principle, expect and accept that this time will come. If you've engaged yourself deeply with the finished piece, you will suffer a bit of depression in letting it go. During this time you might feel enervated and stale. If you're proud of what you've been able to accomplish in the previous piece, you may feel that you can never quite hit that level again. The completed piece will be your best, the result of luck or fate or some unique mingling of circumstance that will happen only once in your life. Or, you may simply feel tired. You may be emotionally and creatively exhausted. The silos of inspiration stand empty. Whatever form your blocked-at-the-new-beginning mindset takes, use the prompts in this chapter to begin again. Some of the prompts speak directly to this mindset, while others offer new ways of beginning that you can use at any stage of your writing life.

Put It On Paper

PROMPT: Here's the easiest prompt in the book—don't write anything. Give yourself a specific amount of time away from writing. When we try to push through exhaustion by using will and determination, we usually end up frustrated and unproductive. Our imaginations need time and care. We have to feed them with new possibilities, new images. And that takes time. However, do give yourself a *specific* amount of time off, based on your natural rhythms and work habits. If you're a writer who needs time to recover and begin thinking about a project before beginning to scribble words on paper, give yourself what you need. If you're a writer who needs less time, who can begin with energy and vigor after only a short pause, honor your ability. If you're not sure how much time you need, set a specific start date anyway and adjust to how you feel when that date arrives. Do set that date. Time off is essential, but too much time erodes the habit of writing that you've worked hard to create, and before long you'll need to develop the habit again. Set the date. Take some time off. Enjoy. Let life wash over you and through you.

PROMPT: Another easy one: Spend a session with a stack of magazines and scissors. Cut out at least ten pictures of people. Cut ten more of events—some type of action, anything from a couple entering a room to firefighters battling a blaze. Keep your piles of people and events separate. Shuffle them a few times. Close your eyes and pick three from the people pile and three from the event pile. Paste them together into a collage and study it. Let your mind begin to draw connections among the pictures. Spend a session exploring these connections and allow a story to develop through those connections.

PROMPT: Go someplace you've never been and don't bring your notebook or tape recorder. The place can be as accessible as a shop in your neighborhood, or it could be a town near where you live. The key is discovery—filling your senses with new information. Keep your senses open. Talk to people. Ask questions. Do whatever it takes to connect with the place. If you're visiting a clothing store, try on a dress or a pair of pants. Touch things. Close your eyes and focus on sounds. When you return home, you can write down your impressions but don't force yourself to write. Our goal here is not research or to fill new pages of our notebooks. Our goal is to feed our imaginations, to experience a fresh environment outside the context of writing.

PROMPT: Visit a museum and spend some time focused on a single exhibit or show. Use the method we discussed in the previous prompt (except for the directive to "touch things"). Your goal is not to record the experience. Instead, linger long enough to interact with the exhibit, studying its nuances and subtleties.

PROMPT: One more visit—spend at least an hour in a natural setting where you've never been before. The place can be as accessible as a park in your town, or you may want to drive into the country. Walk around. Scoop dirt into your hands and feel its texture. Close your eyes and listen to the sounds around you. Linger long enough to connect with the place.

PROMPT: Let's try a variation on picking one from Pile A and one from Pile B. This time, we'll focus on words. Flip at random through a dictionary and write down the first ten concrete nouns you find. You're making a list of things. (On my search I pointed to reef, penguin, concertina, infield, hemp, rain, snorkel, pie, waterhole, cornet.) If your finger falls on a word that's not a concrete noun, find the closest one or flip to a new page. When you have your list, search for ten abstract nouns, words that name ideas, feelings, and beliefs. (On my search I found religion, justice, enthusiasm, outrage, dislike, truth, sentiment, misery, agitation, ambition.) Compiling the second list may take longer than it took you to compile the first one, but stay the course. Allow yourself to enjoy skimming through the dictionary. Linger on words you don't recognize. Write them down on a separate sheet of paper and add them to your vocabulary. When you've finished both lists, write them in two adjacent columns on a single page. Then begin pairing them in various ways. You might try writing sentences using a pair in similes, such as— *Truth is like a snorkel* or *Misery is like a concertina*. Write a page to support your simile, either in an expository or narrative mode. Or you could pair the words in a description, such as *Throughout the evening Abbey played her concertina of misery.*

PROMPT: Pick a place where you've spent time in your life. Draw a map of it, noting the places where various events occurred. They need not be significant events. You might mark, for example, the grocery store near where you lived and chart the route you took from your home to the store. Have fun with the map. Use markers and highlighters of many colors. Allow the process to spark memories of people, situations, events, details. Spend a few sessions writing about this place. If you feel inspired, keep going.

PROMPT: Follow the same process described in the previous prompt but focus on a fictional place or simply allow yourself to fictionalize elements of a place you remember from your life. The key: have fun with it. Go nuts with the map, and when you're ready, begin writing.

PROMPT: Spend several writing sessions paging through reference books, particularly guides to specific subjects, such as trees, historical figures, architecture, transportation vehicles. Writers need to know the names of things, so spending time with reference guides is essential. Also, the names, descriptions and pictures of things can feed your imagination. Write the names that particularly interest you in your notebook.

Use one or two as the basis for a writing session. For example, I opened a reference book and found information about the Hudson Hornet, a car made in the early 1950s. I searched the internet for a bit more information about it, then wrote a sentence in which a character pulls up to a house in a Hudson Hornet. Why is he there? What is the nature of his visit? A quick flip through a guide to birds gave me the Louisiana heron. I opened a guide to Americana and the first entry that caught my eye was Tabasco sauce (which has been bottled and sold since 1868, a fact I didn't know.) And it's bottled in Louisiana, home to the Louisiana heron. Perhaps there's a case of Tabasco sauce in the backseat of that Hudson Hornet as it pulls up to the house. Why is it there? Is it a peace offering brought by the driver to the people who live in the house? And how does a heron figure into the scene? You see where I'm going. Reference guides can give you specific information that can lead to your next piece of writing.

PROMPT: Here's a variation on the previous prompt. Pick a page from a visual dictionary, a reference guide that provides the names of the parts of various things. If you don't have this type of dictionary at home, you can find one in any library. Spend a session writing a short piece in which you use most of the names of the thing you found. If possible, create a scene, dropping the descriptive words in at appropriate intervals rather than simply writing a description in which you use the words.

PROMPT: Let's focus on cutting the cord with the piece you've finished recently by consciously doing the opposite of what you did in that piece. For example, is the finished piece a dark study of character? Freewrite by focusing on humor and action. Is the previous piece set mostly indoors? Freewrite a scene or two set outside. Is the protagonist in the previous piece a solemn introvert? Freewrite about a character who is gregarious.

PROMPT: Did you have a specific place and time for writing the piece you finished recently? If so, make a change for the next few sessions. Create a new routine. You can always return to the old one if it's more convenient, but let's break the old routine for a while.

PROMPT: Try a new form. If the piece you finished recently is a novel, spend a few sessions creating scenes in a play. If you've just finished a play, try a personal essay. If your previous piece focused closely on the lives of a few characters, explore a national issue. If your previous piece was based on a real-life experience, write about an experience that's made up from start to finish.

PROMPT: In the opening of this chapter I mentioned the familiar situation in which a writer, while working on one piece is distracted by interest in a different piece. When he finishes the first piece, however, the new one seems far less interesting than before. The new one existed in our minds mostly as a distraction, a device we create to relieve us from the burden of completing the piece we're writing. If you resisted the urge to hop to the new piece, good for you. If the new piece now doesn't interest you, let it go. If it still interests you but you're feeling blocked at the beginning, schedule the next three writing sessions to work on it. You may be blocked because you're expecting the piece to possess the level of invention and particularity of the previous one, forgetting that achieving that level in the previous one took a long time. Have patience. Allow the new one to find itself, to begin to reveal its own qualities.

PROMPT: If you've been keeping an idea notebook, open to a page at random and point to an entry. Make that entry the focus of your next three sessions. The key is that it's a random choice. There's no pressure to make it a masterpiece, and the choice is not guided by a desire to continue the thread of the piece you've completed recently. It's important, furthermore, to explore the piece in at least three sessions before moving to something else. When we finish a piece that took some time to complete, we tend to hop among a number of new ideas, which is not a bad approach in itself, if you want to play and experiment for a while. However, if you find yourself getting frustrated by beginning a new piece with every session, try spending a little more time on each one and allowing it to grab your interest.

PROMPT: If you're feeling stale, seeing your new ideas as clichés, let's push into that feeling. Begin a piece in which you prove a cliché wrong. First, write a list of a half-dozen clichés, such as "Cheaters never prosper," "Ignorance is bliss," "You get what you pay for," or "A penny saved is a penny earned." Then recall an event or create a fictional event in which a cheater prospers or ignorance is decidedly not bliss.

PROMPT: When we begin a new piece after finishing one, we often feel tired, bored, frustrated, impatient, anxious, or confused. Let's push into what you're feeling by creating a character who is feeling the same way but for different reasons. Give your characters some reasons. If you're writing nonfiction, write about the emotion itself or write about another time in your life when you felt the same way, though not in connection with your writing.

PROMPT: Let's use the final prompts in this chapter to move beyond the previous piece by creating some new situations and conflicts. Write about a character who is by nature an introvert but for some reason is forced to act in an open, friendly way. For example, your introvert is forced to host a reception for his boss and must create a festive atmosphere.

PROMPT: Reverse the previous prompt—your outgoing character is in a situation in which she must be silent and passive, observing the people and action around her rather than leading the action.

PROMPT: Place a character in a place that rubs against the character's nature, where he or she feels exceedingly uncomfortable. The character works very hard to hide or mask the lack of comfort but eventually is exposed.

PROMPT: Make a list of expressions we use to communicate that we're in trouble such as "up a tree," "between a rock and a hard place," "in hot water" "at the end of my rope." Place a character literally in such a place.

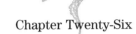

Chapter Twenty-Six

Last Words and Recommendations

My hope in writing this book is that it helps you make your good ideas better and that it helps you finish some projects you had abandoned. The fundamental themes of the book, its basic recommendations, should be clear by now, so I won't repeat them. Except one: Writing is hard. Our first ideas are not always our best ones, and even our best ones require development. They require us to recognize and explore their possibilities, to be willing to change and augment them, to add new ideas to the initial ones. That's how stories in whatever form you write are built.

I opened my earlier book, *The Writer's Idea Book* by saying "Writing is an act of hope," and I still believe that. Writing requires tenacity and faith and the belief that what we write will change us—and the world—in a positive way. Writing offers us a way of understanding ourselves and the world. It develops our capacity for empathy, which is one of the greatest qualities human beings can possess. Writing well requires time and patience, and there's no guarantee that achieving a level of mastery will make you rich or famous or that your gifts will be recognized and appreciated. But if your goal is to achieve a level of mastery in order to reach a new level of empathy and a new level of understanding of your fellow travelers in life, then fame and fortune truly are beside the point.

It's a grand mission you've chosen, and you should take pride in the bravery it takes to choose that mission.

To help us in our mission, many writers have given us great books of advice. Some of them I had the honor to work with as an editor. Others I've met through conferences or through the inevitable connections that exist within the small world of publishing. Others I've not met but have benefited from their books. Having worked for the past twenty years as a teacher of writing, an editor of books on how to write, and as a writer, I've developed a list of favorite books, which I've listed below. No doubt I've left off a few that should be included. Blame my failing memory. But the books below offer more than enough insight into the art and craft of writing to last you a lifetime or two.

The category of writing instruction is a much-maligned one. A couple of years ago an op-ed in the *Wall Street Journal* kindly noted that such books "belong in the 'magic' section of the bookstore, next to 'grand illusions' and 'let's pretend.' " Even those writers who agree to write a supportive blurb for the jacket cover of books by friends and colleagues often preface their remarks with an "at last" and "finally," the implication being that they have combed through hundreds of such books and found them all lacking. I admit that when I went from the university classroom to work at the company that owns Writer's Digest Books I had a similar, and similarly uninformed, prejudice. I believed that such books were useless, a way of tricking the hopelessly untalented into believing they could be the next literary superstar. Of course, I hadn't actually read the books. When I began reading them, I was surprised by the level of useful instruction they offered. No one was telling me I could write a bestseller unless I was willing to learn the craft and study the market. No one was telling me I could write the Great American Novel in fifteen minutes a day. In fact, I found a much greater supply of practical, specific instruction than I found during my years of graduate school. The years of higher education helped me immeasurably in shaping my sensibility and in introducing me to the work of brilliant writers. I am fortunate to have worked with gifted teachers and gifted colleagues. But these books taught me some of the basics that the workshops ignored—

simple things like how to move a character from here to there, why a choice of points of view can work for this but not for that.

As in all categories in the bookstore, some books are better than others. Some are written only for the money. Others are written by writers of some accomplishment who are not gifted teachers. They don't know or understand their audience or simply lack the ability to speak in a specific way about how they do what they do on the page. None of the books will turn their reader from a novice into a master in a few hundred pages. As we've discussed throughout this book, writing is a craft that can be learned, but it requires a certain degree of innate talent, a level of intuition that is more closely connected to art than to craft. It requires passion, the need to express oneself on the page. It requires having something interesting to express. It requires reading. It requires an apprenticeship of hard work, of a number of failures before the first success. If there are dozens of books on the market that tell readers that none of those requirements are necessary, I haven't found them.

You certainly won't find them on the list below. You'll find the advice that will help you reach the next level of mastery. You'll find inspiration. You'll find, as the writers of the *I Ching* say, "like minds." These writers have taken the journey, and their books give us the wisdom learned along the way.

ABC's of Writing Fiction, by Ann Copeland
A Year in the Life, by Sheila Bender
Art and Craft of Playwriting, The, by Jeffrey Hatcher
Art and Craft of the Short Story, The, by Rick DeMarinis
Art of Fiction, The, David Lodge
Art of Fiction, The, John Gardner
Beyond Style, by Gary Provost
Bird by Bird, by Anne Lamott
Creative Nonfiction, by Philip Gerard
Dimwit's Dictionary, The, by Robert Hartwell Fiske, Joseph Epstein
Elements of the Writing Craft, by Robert Olmstead
Eye of the Story, The, by Eudora Welty
Fiction Writer's Workshop, by Josip Novakovich

Forest for the Trees, The: An Editor's Advice to Writers, by
   Betsy Lerner
Lessons from a Lifetime of Writing, by David Morrell
Making Shapely Fiction, by Jerome Stern
Observation Deck, The: A Tool Kit for Writers, by Naomi Epel
On Writing Well, by William Zinsser
Pencil Dancing: New Ways to Free Your Creative Spirit, by
   Mari Messer
Pocket Muse, The, by Monica Wood
Poemcrazy, by Susan Wooldridge
Revising Fiction: A Handbook for Writers, by David Madden
Revision: A Creative Approach to Writing and Rewriting Fiction,
   by David Michael Kaplan
Rhetoric of Fiction, The, by Wayne C. Booth
*Story: Style, Structure, Substance and the Principles of Screenwrit-
   ing,* by Robert McKee
Turning Life into Fiction, by Robin Hemley
What If?, by Anne Bernays and Pamela Painter
Why I Write: Thoughts on the Craft of Fiction, edited by Will Blythe.
Word Painting, by Rebecca McClanahan
Write from Life, by Meg Files
Write Tight, by Bill Brohaugh
Writer's Survival Guide, The, by Rachel Simon
Writing a Book That Makes a Difference, by Philip Gerard
Writing the Breakout Novel, by Donald Maass
Writing in General and the Short Story in Particular, by Rust Hills
Writing Life Stories, by William Roorbach
Writing Past Dark, by Bonnie Friedman
*Writing Personal Essays: How to Shape Your Life Experiences on
   the Page,* by Sheila Bender
Writing the Wave: Inspired Rides for Aspiring Writers, by
   Elizabeth Ayers

Index

Get More of the Best Writing Instruction From Writer's Digest Books!

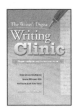

More of the Best Books for Writers!

Lessons From a Lifetime of Writing—Best-selling author David Morrell distills more than 30 years of writing and publishing experience into this single masterwork of advice and instruction, examining everything from motivation to the building blocks of good fiction.
ISBN 1-58297-270-2, paperback, 256 pages, #10917-K

The Pocket Muse—Here's the key to finding inspiration when and where you want it. Hundreds of thought-provoking prompts, exercises and illustrations immediately help you to get started writing, overcome writer's block, develop a writing habit, think more creatively and so much more.
ISBN 1-58297-142-0, hardcover, 256 pages, #10806-K

Snoopy's Guide to the Writing Life—You'll find more than 180 heartwarming and hilarious Snoopy "at the typewriter" comic strips by Charles M. Schulz, paired with 32 delightful essays from a who's who of famous writers, including Sue Grafton, Elmore Leonard and more. These pieces examine the joys and realities of the writing life.
ISBN 1-58297-194-3, hardcover, 192 pages, #10856-K

Writer's Guide to Places—Imbue your settings with authentic detail—the kind of information that only an insider would know! You'll find information on all 50 United States, 10 Canadian provinces, and dozens of intriguing cities.
ISBN 1-58297-169-2, paperback, 416 pages, #10833-K

Novel Voices—Discover a wealth of practical and motivating insight from today's most talented authors. Ernest Gaines, Ha Jin, Melanie Rae Thon, William Gass and more offer the instruction and inspiration you need to create winning fiction that will garner critical and creative success.
ISBN 1-58297-245-1, paperback, 272 pages, #10896-K

Roget's Descriptive Word Finder—Make your work fresher and more evocative with this dictionary/thesaurus of adjectives. It's the key to writing with precision and style.
ISBN 1-58297-170-6, hardcover, 464 pages, #10834-K

These books and other fine Writer's Digest titles are available from your local bookstore or online supplier, or by calling 1-800-448-0915.